Jackie MacD

DEAD MEN WALKING

We would like to dedicate this book to
Clare, Linda, Rhea and Lauren – the women who
make us want to be men!

Dead Men Walking

LEE JACKSON, BAZ GASCOYNE
AND FRIENDS

KINGSWAY PUBLICATIONS
EASTBOURNE

First published 2002
Reprinted 2003

ISBN 1 84291 021 3

Published by
KINGSWAY COMMUNICATIONS LTD
Lottbridge Drove, Eastbourne BN23 6NT, England.
Email: books@kingsway.co.uk

Book design and production for the publishers by
Bookprint Creative Services, P.O. Box 827, BN21 3YJ, England.
Printed in Great Britain.

Contents

Thanks

From Lee . . .

Big thanks to everyone who helped me write this book and has heard me harping on about it for two years – especially people who have given us quotes and help.

Special thanks to Christine and Luisa, who helped make sense of my dictation!

To everyone at Leeds Faith in Schools, thank you for putting up with me and teaching me how to follow Jesus.

Thanks also to everyone at Dayspring Church for letting me be myself. Toby, you are a good lad! Steve, I appreciate your friendship and your honesty. Thanks, Linda, for coming to Leeds!

Thanks to Steve Reilly for trying to understand me and keeping me sharp.

To everyone in Leeds for digging in their heels – God bless you!

Andy A. – you keep me going just by being around and serving God in the way you do.

Justin, Emma, Greg, Matt and Andy have had a significant input into the book. Thanks for being so generous with your time.

Thanks to Mam for everything and to Dad for being my dad! I have learned such a lot from you both.

Most of all I would like to thank all the men I have met who have inspired me and kept me on the straight and narrow, and pushed me into a fuller life with Jesus – especially Justin and Matt, who have been my best friends over many years and have seen all sides of me. And Baz: every time I meet you, you challenge me about my walk with God without even saying a word!

From Baz . . .

To my darling wife, Linda, for all your love, support and encouragement, not just through this project but through the years before we were married and since. 'I still believe the best of you' and thank you for returning the sentiment. I love you more than I've probably told you or shown you.

To Lee, for suggesting the possibility of writing this book together, and the patience he has shown due to my slow typing!

To our friends who have contributed material for this book: we owe you a curry.

To the fantastic people at the Eccles church where I have the privilege of sharing their lives. You are a great bunch of people – keep pursuing God and his ways.

To the Pioneer network that I am involved with personally and as a church. It is so good to know I'm home. What heroes you are!

To my best mate, Steve Halliwell. Thanks for your friendship and love.

To Paul Wakelam, for being such a great friend and role model.

To Roger Ellis, who all those years ago in the early 1980s saw a rough and hurting young man and gave him the time and encouragement to help him become what he is today.

To all the Christians who have had input into my life from that first day in July 1977 – too many to mention but never forgotten. You will be rewarded.

Finally, to God my Father, who has faithfully helped me through my Christian life, and keeps overwhelming me with his outrageous grace.

Preface

When a group of friends (predominantly male) get together to write 'honestly' about important life issues, especially masculinity, the cringe factor could be quite high. Not so with this book. The interplay between story and teaching is done skilfully and energetically. The book is passionate without being pious, hard-hitting without being hurtful, and thought provoking without being tedious.

Lee and Baz approach Christian themes with refreshing candour and with an unselfconscious enquiry which is both disarming and creative. It may not be the first choice for the more sensitive church-based study groups but many, particularly young people and those on the fringe of the church, will find it liberating and engaging.

The Rt Revd Cyril G Ashton
Bishop of Doncaster

Preface

[illegible]

Foreword

Okay, brace yourself.

The boys who wrote this book don't wear sandals. They probably haven't got any fishes on the rear end of their motors, and, if they were to wear a tie, it would probably be looped around their heads. If you felt led to give them a Robin Reliant, they'd torch it.

Their book is just possibly about to scare the living daylights out of you. If you're looking for a warm, fuzzy, happy little book of 'precious-moments' encouragement that will exhort you to be a thoroughly nice Christian chap, put this epistle down right now! This book is raw, rude, offensive, gripping and occasionally gut-wrenching, with an honesty that will leave you breathless and a call that could seriously mess up your life – in the best possible way.

Whether I agree with it all or endorse it totally as a chunk of print is a secret. But I do know these two kingdom thugs quite well. They are as sold out and committed to God as anyone you'll ever find. They've been through some rather tough stuff and still believe that there's a God (which is helpful). They don't just talk about *Braveheart* types, but are wildly passionate about waking men up to discover real masculinity.

Our culture has swallowed a troughful of trash when it comes to being a real man. Planet Chap is filled with blokes who have been drip-fed a consistently dull diet of junk about what it means to be authentically male. Perhaps that's why there's such a need for this brash alarm call.

So I warmly welcome their contribution, and invite you to have your hair stand on end as you read it. Besides, the last book I read that was written specifically for men was called *Maximum Manhood* – sounds seriously intimidating to me . . .

Jeff Lucas

Introduction

Alex Buchanan came to preach at St Albans Vineyard Church in the UK a few years ago and said that he can judge the effectiveness of a church by seeing how many men there can 'wield a sword'! I thought about many of the Christian men I have known over the years and wondered how many of them would be able to pick up a sword, never mind wield it as if their life depended on it!

When I was at junior school in Billingham (in the north east of England) I used to go after school to my Nanna Jackson's house, which wasn't very far away. My memory is a little faint, but I think my granddad was still working at the time. He was a shipyard worker and people say this is one of the hardest jobs you can do. I remember him coming in from work and undoing his boots on the kitchen stool. He just seemed a genuine man to me: he worked hard, his hands were rough, and he often looked tired and worn out, but there was something attractive about him simply because he was a 'real' man. I really looked up to him and enjoyed spending time with him. And to be honest, he had more masculinity than many of the people I have met who are supposedly 'living life to the full'. Sadly he died before I became a teenager.

When I was a teenager I was at a theological college with my mam and dad, I met a lot of interesting characters. Many of them were great, but my lasting impression is of tall, skinny, intellectual, nutcutlet-eating vegetarians who didn't really have much relevance to society! Mr Bean in sandals, socks and a Wallace and Gromit T-shirt is always an image that comes to mind!

Then a friend of mine found this book called *Real Men Don't Eat Quiche* by Bruce Feirstein (who is a James Bond scriptwriter), and that kind of summed it up for me. Throughout my Christian experience as a teenager, every Christian event I went to provided candles and . . . *a nice bit of quiche.*

'A predominantly middle-class church is probably seen in the same way as ballet – something for well-off people and not for real men.' (Tony Watkins of Damaris commenting on the film *Billy Elliot*)

This book is based partly around the deep theological truth that real men don't eat quiche! As I thought more about my childhood I realised there were very few Christian men who actually inspired me. Why? I was attracted more to the 'realness' of non-Christian men as I grew up, and since then I have been seeking genuine male relationships in my life. And when I find them I know straight away . . .

I was once at a youth event as a DJ, and while getting some chips I started chatting to this guy called Ian. It was one of those conversations where you really start to connect with somebody. I realised that I had a lot in common with him, and saw that he was genuinely trying to live his life, fighting his way to Jesus. It was exciting for me because I hadn't met many people like that, especially in the north. He now lives on the south coast, and one of the reasons he moved there was to be in a church where he could have real relationships. I meet him, Baz and a few other real men I respect, every year now at a conference, where we have a great laugh together. And to be honest it is one of the highlights of my year. (I know I sound a bit sad, but it is true!)

It was as Baz and I talked together that we realised maybe we had something to say just by sharing our lives, and that is the reason for this book. It is not going to give you all the answers – you may agree with some things, you may disagree with others, some things might wind you up and you might throw the book against the wall. That's fine with us, so long as it sparks off some dialogue, some discussion, or gets some brain matter moving, because we need simply to talk to each other, to let each other know about our hearts, our dreams, our visions.

John Eldridge says in the amazing book *Wild at Heart*, 'The Christian world has made the pinnacle of Christian maleness to be a "nice bloke".' But I am more attracted by someone like the couch potato Jim Royle from the TV series *The Royle Family*, or a 7′ 1″ Shaquille O'Neal who can dunk the ball hard in somebody's face, than I am by most Christian men I have met. I want to learn how to live my life, to harness my passions and my aggressions, to give everything I can in relationships, and hopefully through some of this reality actually start to stem the flow of men getting out of the church (or, even worse, getting apathetic in the church!).

One of my basketball heroes is Vince Carter. He can fly to the hoop like no one I have ever seen before. He said, 'I just want to be Vince Carter.' It sounds simple but there is quite a lot in that. I simply want to be Lee Jackson, not to be pushed in a box and have my gifts caged up because they are not seen as relevant to church life. I want to shout and scream, I want to play basketball hard, I want to be known as a grafter, as someone who doesn't give up, as a good DJ, a good dad, a good husband, ultimately a good follower of Jesus. If you spend your life in Christian culture and are not too careful, your real self, your true masculinity, can disappear – or certainly it will be implied that it is not important.

'Spirituality has been framed and Christian men no longer know what it means to be masculine.' (John Eldridge, *Wild at Heart*)

I was asked to do a men's day for a church in Yorkshire, and as I shared my heart for a couple of sessions the men there genuinely responded. At the end, a 20-year-old lad came up to me and said, 'I just want to thank you for being real with me. I have been in the church for years and that is the first time someone has spoken to me and not talked down to me. You made it make sense.' I was shocked that this lad had had to wait so long for a man to speak his language, and we wonder where all the men are! They have legged it – simple as that!

This book is about getting real with each other, so here's me getting real with you . . .

I was in the waiting room with all the other men embarrassed to be there. We all giggled nervously and a few told forced jokes to help ease their nerves. But mainly it was silent, everyone realising they were putting their manhood on the line – literally! One flinch from the scalpel and it would all be over! All our clothes and status had disappeared as soon as we put on those starched hospital gowns that always open when you don't want them to!

Everyone was nervous, most had come with friends or partners, and the bloke opposite me was holding his wife's hand tightly. The surgeon came out and started to explain the operation to us in friendly but graphic detail. Then I had the feeling I have always dreaded, and before I knew it a male nurse was bringing me round as I was slouched on Clare's knee! I realised that my brief exit from the world had broken the ice among these macho men; they were all genuinely concerned for me, asking if I was all right and maybe starting to wonder whether I knew something they didn't! In that brief moment of concern I saw something of the real men, and not the '*me*, *my* castle, *my* car, *my* job and *my* barbecue men' we all pretend to be.

This book is a cry from the heart for genuine masculinity to rise up in the church. The chapters are deliberately short and packed full of quotes and information, as well as true stories about things we have gone through. It is designed to be a description of real lives rather than in-depth theoretical theology.

In the process of writing this book we contacted loads of people we know and asked them for a few comments they might want to share with other men. Some of them were happy for the chance to let off a bit of steam and open their hearts, and their comments are interspersed throughout. I'll give you first names in most cases, but you'll have to guess their second names!

If this book does nothing other than encourage you to be real with other men, then it has served its purpose.

Lee Jackson

P.S. For further information, please visit our website at www.deadmenwalking.net

1

A Lesson in the Three Rs

LEE JACKSON

'You can never establish a personal relationship without opening up your own heart.' (Paul Tournier)

After three years of working for Leeds Faith in Schools as the only schools worker in Leeds, we eventually had enough money to employ our second worker – very exciting for me, the famous Lone Ranger! When the applications came in we sifted through them in the normal way, except for one application. It was not on the typed form like all the others; it was a colourful creative CV with photos and info crammed into its badly photocopied pages. As I glanced through it, there was a phrase that stuck out and persuaded me that we had found our next worker. It said: 'All youth work is based on the three Rs – Relationships, Relationships, Relationships.'

What a statement! I later found out that it had been written in the middle of the night in a haze of caffeine, but aren't a lot of good things? (Whether or not it's an original thought is difficult to tell!) The three Rs are not only applicable to youth work but to the whole of our lives. Think about it – what is more important than relationships? Our relationships with our wife or girlfriend, children, family and friends are the most important things in our lives.

Then there is our relationship with God: even if we don't follow him we still have a relationship with him. God is 'three in one', so even at the heart of God relationships are key. When Jesus came to earth he spent his time with a few rough men and women, trying to build relationships with them and make a difference in their lives. He could have chosen to ride on a cloud or live as a hermit – you can choose to be anything if you are God!

The evangelist J. John spoke at a young evangelists' conference I was invited to. I can't remember much of what he said, except for one of his now-famous phrases: 'The main thing is to keep the main thing the main thing!' The main thing for us is relationships. Nothing is more important, and nothing comes close to matching it. The whole of this book is based on this simple piece of common sense. Putting relationships first in our lives means that everything else falls into its rightful place. Let's face it – all men think they have healthy relationships, but how many of us really have?

Honesty

To move towards deeper relationships with people we need to develop a greater sense of honesty and realness. I used to work at the Crown Court in Leeds (I thought I'd start as a criminal and work my way up!). As an admin officer, I shuffled paper from one side of my desk to the other, and then went home. In the mornings there used to be a ritual that drove me mad: it was the 'say hello to everyone game'. Everyone used to say, 'Hello, good morning, how are you?' but no one ever replied honestly or ever listened for a reply! 'Yeah, fine thanks' or 'Fair to middling' was the only response. Some people even answered the question when you hadn't asked them! I love giving people more information than they want: 'Well, I feel a bit tired actually and I am concerned about my relationship with my wife, and my dog has fleas.' You have never seen people run so fast. We need to get real with each other and stop covering over the cracks with our English barriers. I must admit, though, there is a fine line between being honest and becoming a constant whinger. We will have to find the balance somewhere.

'Football was invented because men have got nothing to say to their mates.' (Ben Elton)

For men the depth issue is easy to push further – try steering conversations away from football, cars and 'what I would do if I won the lottery', and see what happens. Beyond the banter and football talk there is often a man who is lonely and craves true friendship. I know that from my own life. I still have feelings of loneliness and these feelings are shared by some of my (honest) friends. Is the Internet so popular with men because you only share the bits you want to share in emails and selective chat room relationships?

Purpose-driven?

There is a problem with a rediscovery of relationships, and that is so-called purpose-driven friendships (a term used in management training and certain churches). I have no doubt as to the validity of such relationships, but we have to balance things up. Do we deliberately spend time with people for no reason other than to spend time with them? As someone who enjoys networking, it is a pressure not to talk about work, but when I don't it feels great just to connect with someone. As we understand one another more, God makes the right connections anyway – bonus! The other day my friend Simon said to me, 'Let's get together, Lee; I feel as if we're drifting apart.' We had both been busy and he was right – we needed time together, not just for the sake of our work but just for our sake.

> Christian churches of all kinds, of course, major on 'preaching up' commitment – to our marriages, to our friendships, to Christ and (by no means least) commitment to those churches . . . Nevertheless, the fact remains that, in the cultural climate of the West, our commitment to one another is very low indeed. (Meic Pearse and Chris Matthews, *We Must Stop Meeting Like This*, Kingsway Publications)

An influential church and youth leader once 'announced' to me that he had chosen me as his friend – we had one meal together and now he only talks to me when he needs something! Mmmm.

Since God has pressed on me the importance of relationships with others, I have spent time writing more emails and my phone bill has gone up. So it is not without its costs, but the results are worth it.

I coach and play basketball in school and I spent a considerable time with one group of sixth formers who formed a team, playing basketball with them, organising trips, breaking up fights at their parties and just hanging out with them over the summer holidays. Now they have left school, they still keep in touch, and some of them even train with my team now, which is great. All the time I spent getting them back together and checking if they were all right has paid off with, I hope, friendships for many years to come. No, they are not all sold out, born-again Christians, but I have a special friendship with some of them and they are not embarrassed to be seen with 'that bloke who did the religious assemblies'.

Fragrance

But what happens if people don't like you? I used to be in a basketball team where most of the members seemed to hate me. I left in the end because of it. I had helped them, been a faithful member of the team but, for whatever reason, they hated me. They loved it when I missed a shot or got fouled – it was weird. I went back recently to play against them (two-and-a-half years after I had left) and they still heckled me and were delighted when we lost the match. Some people you will never connect with. I can honestly get on with most people, but these guys simply hated me. Then I read a bit from the Bible that freaked me out:

> Through us, he brings knowledge of Christ. Everywhere we go, people breathe in the exquisite fragrance. Because of Christ, we give off a sweet scent rising to God, which is recognized by those on the way of salvation—an aroma redolent with life. But those on the way to destruction treat us more like the stench from a rotting corpse. This is a

> terrific responsibility. Is anyone competent to take it on? No—but at least we don't take God's Word, water it down, and then take it to the streets to sell it cheap. We stand in Christ's presence when we speak; God looks us in the face. We get what we say straight from God and say it as honestly as we can. Does it sound like we're patting ourselves on the back, insisting on our credentials, asserting our authority? Well, we're not. Neither do we need letters of endorsement, either to you or from you. You yourselves are all the endorsement we need. Your very lives are a letter that anyone can read by just looking at you. Christ himself wrote it—not with ink, but with God's living Spirit; not chiseled into stone, but carved into human lives—and we publish it. (2 Corinthians 2: 14–17 *The Message*)

Maybe I was the smell of death to these blokes. (Or maybe they just hated me!) These verses have stayed with me as a reminder of what a responsibility we have to try to maintain good relationships with all people, but sometimes you just have to shake the dust from your feet and move on. However, I do believe this is a last and not a first response, as some people seem to think.

I have been a sweet smell to some people though, you will be glad to know. I used to buy a sandwich on the way to work every Friday, and one day the shop owner said she was selling up the business and moving to France. We had always had a laugh together and I was sad to see her go. On the last day I gave her a hug and wished her well, and to my amazement she said that there was something different about me and she had always enjoyed serving me. Obviously the way I ordered sandwiches was somehow different to other people's sandwich orders! The fragrance of Christ again?

Carry on loving . . .

I am a big comedy fan and I love the old Ealing comedies and the early *Carry On* films. But amazingly many of these comedians were paranoid, mean, self-destructive and lonely people. How people who are so gifted manage to destroy the people around them I will never understand. In all the biographies and documentaries of comedians, there are only one or two who are always talked of very highly. Hattie Jacques (the matron in the *Carry On* films) is one of these people. She was a true friend to the greatest collection of outcasts in TV history – the *Carry On* cast. I am never going to be rich in money terms, so maybe I will not be seen as a success in many people's eyes, but I genuinely hope people will talk about me as a person who cared about relationships and not just a man who achieved a lot at the expense of others.

'Most men's meetings I've been to are about as intimate as a GP's waiting room.' (Simon Hall)

Relational church

The emergence in recent years of cell (small group) church is very exciting, and I desperately want it to work, especially for men, as it is probably our last hope of truly reaching our lost people group. Once you get a taste of genuine relationships in and out of church life, there is no going back. Anonymous meetings and shallow friendships stick out like a sore thumb when you have seen and experienced glimpses of the real thing.

Get real

1. Arrange a meeting with someone you work with, for no reason other than to talk to them.
2. Answer honestly when someone you know asks you how you are.
3. When you ask people how they are, wait to hear an answer.
4. Get a cheap phone call package and make that call you keep putting off.
5. When you are filling up your diary, remember the three Rs.
6. Talk to your non-Christian friends about your weaknesses as well, so they know you are not superhuman and you want a real relationship with them.
7. If number 6 does not apply to you, then get some non-Christian friends!

LONELY?

'The open discussion of loneliness is the most taboo subject in the world. Forget sex, politics or religion or even failure, loneliness is what clears out a room.' (Douglas Coupland, from the book *Miss Wyoming*)

If we are brutally honest with each other, we will admit most men are lonely people. We talk about football, cars and girls – but don't get much further.

If suicide is the second biggest killer of young men, why don't we talk about it?

2

And Whatever Did Happen to the Heroes?

BAZ GASCOYNE

The dictionary meaning of hero is: 'Any man noted for feats of courage or nobility of purpose; especially one who has risked or sacrificed his life: a person who is greatly admired because of his special achievements or contributions in some event, field or period.'

The Stranglers sang: 'Whatever happened to all the heroes? . . . No more heroes any more.' There is a cry from society today for heroes who will not let down their followers or supporters.

There has never been a more important time than today for young boys, teenagers and men to have heroes; heroes who are going to be good role models and not cause disappointment and disillusionment by their behaviour.

The heroes of the political and religious arenas have not escaped media coverage of their misdemeanours in the past, and rightly so.

It was while at junior school that I first experienced putting someone in the category of a hero. The person involved was a schoolteacher named Mr Hardy. He was everything I did not have in a father. First, he was there every day. Not like mine, who left to live in Africa. Second, he was funny and was very encouraging to me. He had the ability to make you feel good about yourself even when you were struggling with some aspect of work. He was our football coach, and not only knew about coaching but could play as well. He was a great teacher and could make the most boring subject sound interesting.

The one thing he really got me excited about was the stories and characters in the Bible: Moses, David, Joseph, Elijah, Jesus . . . It was no wonder I won the school Scripture prize that year. What was so amazing was that I became a charismatic Christian before I became a Christian. Let me explain: every time we had an assembly and sang a hymn or a song I would start to jump up and down with excitement while singing. The hymn that caused the biggest stir in me was 'O Jesus I have promised'. The staff and other pupils used to look on with puzzlement and amusement. I don't know why Jesus had become a hero to me, especially when I did not know him at that time. Mr Hardy had a great way of making the Bible and the characters come alive.

Why was this teacher a hero of mine? It was because he had the ability to bring out the best in people. He listened to them, encouraged them and believed in them. Even when he disciplined you, you believed it was for your benefit.

Senior school was a great time for me. I was into football in a big way, as well as other sports. If I could have done PE all day I would have been in my element. I did have sporting heroes of my day but knew I would never meet them or emulate their achievements. At school there was a pupil I looked up to. He was a fifth former when I started the school, and his name was Gordon. I had met Gordon during the summer holidays when a few of us went to play football with some of the staff and pupils from the senior school. He was supposed to be one of the hardest boys in the school. There was a rumour that some of the staff wanted him to be head boy due to the respect he had from the other pupils (which was not down to his ability to use his fists but down to his character). However, the head and deputy put a halt to that due to him not being what was expected from a head boy. Where do we see that happen time and again? I'll give you a clue – six letters, the first two being CH and the last two being CH. What's missing? UR! Gordon was an all-round sportsman who always gave 100 per cent in everything he did.

When I was 13, I was asked to sign for the under-18s football club, Whessoe Juniors, who played in the Darlington and District Youth League. Gordon was the captain. The manager asked me to bring my boots along for the last game of the season, a cup final. I was to be one of the substitutes, but did not expect to get a game. With about 15 minutes to go to the end of the game the manager shouted to me to get warmed up. The next thing I knew I was on the same field as one of my heroes.

I had been on the pitch about one minute when I got my first touch of the ball. I also got a good clobbering from one of the opponents and the next thing I knew I was lying on the grass in agony.

I was not sure if the pain I could feel was coming from my legs or back or both. I have never been hit by a bulldozer before, but I'm sure this came close to what it might feel like. To be honest, I didn't want to get up – it would have been easier to get carried off. The next thing I heard was Gordon saying, 'Don't worry, I'll get him back. But now get up and don't let the bastard see you are hurt – show him what you can do.' Slowly but with determination I got up and started to jog to run off the pain.

Sure enough, true to his word, Gordon returned the compliment to the guy who fouled me. He did it in such a way that no foul was given but the guy needed to be carried off the pitch and substituted. A quick wink and smile from Gordon to me said it all; he had looked out for me. Although I can't agree now with what he did, boys and men are looking for heroes who will protect, encourage and support them in all they do.

One staff member at senior school made an immediate impression on me, and that was my house master, Miles Burnidge. I never admitted this to my mates, but I admired him for the way he led the house, taught and encouraged people. I remember in one assembly in my first year after our house had won the school athletics day, Mr Burnidge was making a speech of how proud he was of everybody who took part, including those who supported the athletes. He went on to say how one pupil had made such a positive contribution to the rest of the team, not just by winning their four events but by the way they supported, encouraged and motivated others in the team during the sports day and before in the training days. I, like many others, assumed he was talking about Gordon. Imagine the feeling of amazement when he called out my name to come and collect the award of the house athletics colours – the first time ever a first year had been given this award in the school. I could not have felt better!

Miles was very good at motivating the pupils. He seemed to know just what each pupil needed to feel special and appreciated. He had certainly done this for me during that assembly. He was very soon to become another one of my heroes.

'Every adult has a responsibility to be a role model or hero to at least one child.' (Brenda Sanson)

I wonder if both of the teachers mentioned above would agree with this statement? Whether or not they would, they were certainly good role models to me, and I'm almost sure I was not the only one who felt the same.

Brenda Sanson goes on to say, 'Our children need to know that the people we see as heroes do not need to score the winning basket or goal. Our heroes are the people we meet every day of our lives. These are the people who have courage and give unselfishly to others' (from the website at www.unb.ca). This is definitely what I experienced at school. These men were not famous but just ordinary men who obviously loved teaching, showing this by the way they related to the pupils, and in their ability to help others, no matter what background the pupils had come from.

I once heard Gerald Coates say, 'Honour those who have made an impact on your lives and have enhanced them.' These two teachers had done that in my life, so I decided to honour them by inviting them to my wedding with their wives. During my speech at the reception, in front of 200 other guests, I thanked them for being real heroes and for the positive impact they had made in my life during my early years and as a teenager. I hope one day someone could say the same of me.

It is very interesting as you get older and look back on your life, to see which people have been heroes and role models to you.

When I became a Christian at the age of 17, Jesus became one of my heroes and later *the* Hero. As I discovered more about Jesus, I knew that he is what a real hero is about: sacrificial loving and giving without demanding anything in return for himself.

Last year someone came up to me and said, 'Baz, I just want you to know you are one of my heroes.' I often wondered what it must be like to be famous and be someone's hero. Well, I'm not famous and never will be, but to be told you are someone's hero is quite frightening. I wondered why he had said this. What were the qualities in my life that caused him to see me as a hero? Did I deserve such a position? Instead of feeling excited or even big headed, I started to feel fear, curiosity and unrest. I felt afraid of letting him down in the future. What should I do? What would you do? This was so unexpected and had come from such an unlikely source. Having heroes is one thing, but being a hero is quite another.

Two other men also became my heroes when I was younger. One was my old Boys' Brigade officer and the other was my youth leader. The Brigade officer was John Lawrence. He was a real gentleman, who had so much patience; a very devout and holy man of God. Between the ages of 11 and 15 I attended the 1st Darlington Battalion of the Boys' Brigade, and had a great time with a lot of my friends. Unfortunately peer pressure affected teenagers in the 70s just like it does today. Some bright spark at the BB Headquarters in London had this wonderful idea of changing the uniform. The old uniform consisted of school trousers, shirt and blazer, with black tie and shoes, and a white sash, belt and cap, which you got from the BB. It was amazing how much pride we took in wearing this and how much effort was put into cleaning it for inspection each week. So when our captain informed us the uniform was to change and showed us what the new one looked like, I don't think he or the other officers expected such a reaction. There was nearly a riot! The problem was that the new uniform was a blue shirt with a white tassel on one of the shoulders. It was too feminine for the likes of us 15-year-old northerners. It was OK for those southerners, but not for us.

One lad commented, 'If we have to wear that, we'll all leave,' and this was echoed by a large 'Yeah'. The officers were quite shocked by the response but tried to talk us round to just trying these uniforms. However, true to our words and true to the effect of peer pressure, we had all left within two weeks. It must have been hard for the officers, especially after giving so much of their time to us over the years, to see about 15 young boys leave over something as petty as a new uniform. I had been involved for four years and others a lot longer. But boys will be boys.

Seven years later, while home from college for Christmas, I once again bumped into John Lawrence. I went with my friends to a local Anglican church on Christmas Eve. This was the church I had to go to once a month for Brigade Sunday. This time I was there out of choice, because the Methodist church we were part of did not have a service on Christmas Eve.

I cannot recall anything about the service. At the end of the service I was greeted with a huge smile and handshake from John. He looked genuinely pleased to see me, and enquired what I was doing now. When I informed him I had become a Christian and was attending Bible college, he could not stop smiling and told me that he had prayed for my friends and me to become Christians every week since the day we left the BB. This is when John became a hero in my life. What a man of God! What a saint! What a hero! He had prayed for me faithfully for seven years before he discovered I had become a Christian. He told me that evening he would continue to pray for me now that I was living for God.

Every member has to learn the object of the Boys' Brigade and recite it to the captain. When you can do this you receive a badge to wear on your blazer lapel. The object of the BB is: 'The advancement of Christ's kingdom among boys and the promotion of habits, obedience, reverence, discipline, self-respect and all that tends towards a true Christian manliness.' It took me three weeks and probably four attempts before I could recite it fully to the captain and receive my badge. I thought I would never be able to do it. It took seven years of faithfully praying for me before John discovered that his prayers had been answered. The object was for me to experience for myself God and his outrageous grace. That is why he was a hero to me.

Another man to deserve such an accolade was my former youth leader, Bill Brown. When we used to meet at his house for youth group every week I would watch Bill closely, especially when we were worshipping. Every time we began to sing songs or hymns to God, Bill would get off his chair and kneel on the floor, and tears would begin to flow down his cheeks as he sang and prayed. At first I found this rather weird and a bit scary, but later I realised that Bill knew how much God loved him and what Jesus had done for him. Every time we sang 'Blessed assurance' we knew Bill would end up crying. Interestingly, when I sang

'O Jesus I have promised' at my wedding a similar thing happened to me as I realised the immensity of God's love and how he had rescued me from a road of destruction. How we need to see more men crying in times of worship, prayer and fellowship with others as they allow their emotions to be touched by the Spirit of God.

Bill was in his late fifties when I first met him and his wife Ann. They were a great godly couple, whose house was open any time of the day. When I look back at Bill's life I see a man who was passionate about God and his word and sharing that word with others. Bill was a Methodist local preacher. He was very radical in the ways he chose to communicate to people about Jesus. He would often take young people with him from the youth group to help him with the service. He once took two friends of mine with him to a church he was speaking at. Both Shirley and Ken were gifted people. Shirley had an amazing singing voice and Ken was an excellent artist. So while Bill preached, Ken would paint what Bill was talking about, and when he had finished his sermon Shirley would get up and sing a song in her beautiful soul voice. This was in the late 1970s, before anyone had heard a talk about cultural relevance at Spring Harvest or the like.

One time Ann and Bill had arranged for the youth group to go round for a meal at their house. As the group waited for the food to be brought into the room, Bill brought in a huge turkey dish and placed it on the table, with strict instructions for us not to touch the dish or lift the lid until the rest of the food had been brought in. After about two to three minutes one of the group members decided to look under the turkey dish. Bill and Ann were waiting patiently outside the room, knowing that curiosity would get the better of someone. The lid was lifted and the contents revealed a dish full of feathers, which gradually started to come to life! The more frantic this young person became in his attempt to get them back on the dish the more they spread all over the room. As the whole group began desperately trying to help hide the evidence of what he had done, Bill and Ann walked into the room, to the horror of the group. Expecting a lecture on doing what you are told, the young people were amazed at Bill and Ann's response. Bill got his Bible, read a few verses and then went on to talk about temptation and the consequences of sin. That certainly got their attention! I only had Bill as a youth leader a few years before he died suddenly one Good Friday at the age of 61. A great day for Bill to go and be with the Lord, but a very sad day for Ann, Fraser, their son, and their family, as well as the many people who had the privilege of knowing this loving and godly man.

We probably all have Christian heroes of faith like Booth, Finney, Wesley, Spurgeon, Taylor, Livingstone, Edwards, Moody, Seymour, Luther-King, Lake, Wimber, Watson and Wigglesworth. But after reading the stories of these men, you may have been reminded of others who have been influential in your life and deserve to be called heroes. Here is a list of some of the men still alive today who are my heroes. Some you will have heard of and others you won't, but they have all made a mark on my life: Dave France, Paul Wakelam, Steve Halliwell, John Archer, Steve Lowton, Tim Sokell, Ken Anderson, Roger Ellis, Gerald Coates, Jeff Lucas, Robert Mason, Roger Forster, Peter Nodding, Steve Chalke, Gary Gibbs, John Scotland, Phil Wall and Pete Greig.

All these men, plus others, have made an impact on my life, either by the love they have shown me, the encouraging words they have spoken to me or the words I've read from books or heard from talks by them which have challenged and provoked me to become more like Jesus. I value too the time and friendship they have given me to various degrees. They are heroes for the way they serve and love the greatest Hero ever to have walked this earth – Jesus.

Questions

1. Who were your childhood heroes? Why?
2. Who are your biblical heroes?
3. Who are your modern-day heroes of faith?
4. What qualities do you see in them that you admire?
5. Do you think it's right to have heroes as a Christian?
6. How would you cope if someone informed you that you were their hero?

ROLE MODELS

I think that for too long the church in general has promoted stereotypes and role models for men instead of allowing men to be individuals and to express themselves freely. The role models that have been forced upon women in churches are being exposed these days, but the subject of stereotypes for men has never been fully explored.

(Ann)

3
Braveheart
Lee Jackson

'You can't escape it – there is something wild in the heart of every man.' (John Eldredge, *Wild at Heart*)

I was at the UK Pioneer leaders conference in 1997. It was a great conference and I don't say that very often! I spent time with my friends and did a couple of mad things to keep boredom from the door. Behind the conference stage were individual 15′ polystyrene letters spelling out R-E-V-I-V-A-L. This was too good an opportunity for me to miss. So one night when everyone had gone to bed (the Christian time being about 10 pm!), we moved the letters around and put some on top of each other so that it spelt V-E-R-A. The best thing was that Gerald Coates, the Pioneer team leader, thought it was a well-known practical joker who had done it and he went through an elaborate 20-minute fake trial and conviction of this innocent man who was carried out of the auditorium by six big lads. I feel better now confessing that!

But apart from the practical jokes, the humour and

passion at that conference was just amazing. I remember pushing through with God in a few unusual ways and also just having a good laugh with him. We had times of ministry that were great fun and very meaningful to a lot of people.

Apart from the practical jokes, that conference had an amazing effect on my life. During one of the meetings, a group of men from River Church came on the stage with a four-foot sword from the film *Braveheart*. They explained how the film had affected them as they studied it as a church and a youth group. That night was the first time I had heard the famous prayer cry of 'come on', which is now featured on the 24-7prayer.com website, and which people have even preached on. These guys shared their hearts about *Braveheart*, and then they just screamed at the tops of their voices and went into a real war cry. It stirred something up in me that night and I knew I would never be the same again. And when I watched the film, God spoke to me about passion, aggression and prayer. A film has never affected me so much.

> We must press beyond the realm of theory and beyond simply discovering good practice to an encounter with the Lord who trains us for war (Judges 3:10; Psalm 144:1) There is an anointing that we can receive from him that will break the passivity within us and get us ready for war (Joel 2:11; 3:9–16) He is looking for a fight! . . . It is important, as we press in on God, that we are not simply warfare orientated. Worship of Jesus is the highest call, yet worship and warfare are not in opposition, for in Psalm 149 we see that the expression of warfare was birthed in the place of intimacy. (Martin Scott, *Sowing Seeds of Revival*)

It appears to me that the film industry has changed over the last few years and *Braveheart* is definitely a result of that. Traditionally most male action characters are just plain macho with bad attitudes to women and anyone else. It is hard to connect with them and even feel sorry for them. James Bond is the obvious example of this, although he does seem to be getting better with age. He gathers gadgets, kills the baddies and makes love to innumerable women who submit to his charms and bow to his superior masculinity. Thank God for the Judi Dench character 'M' (Bond's boss) who managed to be feminine, strong and certainly wouldn't end up in bed with him! Since *Braveheart*, of course, there are other films, like *Gladiator* and *Fight Club*, that could also be studied in this way (see Resources). *Braveheart* is a film of warfare and intimacy.

'It's not just that a man needs a battle to fight, he needs someone to fight for.' (John Eldredge, *Wild at Heart*)

The film *Braveheart* created a big stir among fans of film, and it has also rekindled something of Scottish nationality in a positive and negative way. There are *Braveheart* websites, message boards, fan clubs, and even talk of a *Braveheart* conference where different people come to explain how the film has affected their lives. If that happens I would love to share how God spoke to me through this film, which may be a bit of a surprise to some of the Scottish National Party!

Once I had seen the sword that the guys from River Church had brought, I just knew I had to have one. It is a hand-and-a-half sword, which is very heavy and definitely the real thing! Someone must have overheard me saying how much I wanted this sword because an envelope arrived with £125 in cash, which was the right amount for it, and a note which said 'a sword for the Lord and for Gideon' (Judges 7: 20).

'We have no great war, our great war is a spiritual war' (From the film *Fight Club*)

It certainly causes a few reactions when I walk into a conference with a four-foot sword! Unfortunately, over the last couple of years, there have been attacks with swords in churches, so I have had to hide it a little bit more than I would like to because I don't want people to think I have got a major psychiatric problem! When I pray for people with my sword it has truly been amazing (and definitely keeps their attention!). I prayed with a senior church leader once at a conference and put the sword into his hands as he kept his eyes closed. As he opened his eyes after we had prayed for a while, he was amazed to see this sword in his hand. He had bought himself a *Braveheart* poster to go above his desk, had seen visions of the sword and just knew it was right for him to pick it up and to use it to pray with. Please dig into the film and let God speak to you.

Here are some study notes on *Braveheart* which you can either do yourself, or use as a group after watching the film. These notes formed part of River Church (Maidstone, UK) leadership training a couple of years ago.

1. What does the story of the film tell us about Wallace?
   - He had a period of training
   - He was recognised as a leader by his peers
   - He didn't cling to 'privileges'

- He was not interested in committees
- He was prepared to die for what he believed in
- No compromise
- Honesty
- Aggressive, even wild
- Prophetic? ('I see strength in you . . .' to the Queen)
- Strategic – not just raw aggression
- Pushed others out (e.g. Robert the Bruce); happy to get behind others
- He died and others took on the battle

2. What was Jesus like and can we see these qualities in the film?
   - A man who lost the comforts of home
   - Came into a lifestyle that was alien to him
   - Didn't crave recognition – was totally secure
   - Didn't just talk – used action
   - No compromise
   - Didn't cling to privileges
   - Rejected the institutions of the day
   - Was honest
   - Was aggressive, even wild
   - Called a radical
   - Upset political stability of the day
   - Was totally subversive
   - Prophetic
   - Trained others up
   - Died for a principle – freedom for the world

3. In the following quote from screenwriter, Randall Wallace, try substituting the word *gospel* for *film*:

Every tale has a message; in what it elevates or attacks, in what it uplifts or denies, every story makes its point.

This film stands upon the affirmations of honour and courage, of faithfulness to the promises of the heart. It is a story built on the history of a man who served these values more than himself, and whose life confronts us with the belief that to put such things above life is life itself.

The making of *Braveheart* has been an act of devotion. Those who have served the soul of this film have, I think, been changed by it. When we have felt unable and unworthy of the attempt to tell such a story, it has made our hearts brave enough to try.

4. Now read Isaiah 53.

5. What does it take to be a William Wallace?
   - Discipline
   - Cost / sacrifice
   - Servanthood
   - Discipleship
   - Endurance
   - Strategy
   - Passion
   - Aggression / power

6. Can you think of any more parallels between Wallace and Jesus than are mentioned here?

7. What does the film teach us about the following:
   - The real heart of a man
   - Church life
   - Living
   - Dying

- Destiny
- Our jobs
- Family

8. Also check out 2 Samuel 23: 8–12 – are there any parallels with William Wallace there?

You can find lots of study resources for films and contemporary culture at the London Institute of Contemporary Christianity www.licc.org.uk and www.damaris.org. Both of these are excellent Christian websites that connect with the culture we live in.

RISK

To laugh is to risk looking a fool
To weep is to risk appearing sentimental
To reach out for another is to risk involvement
To show feelings is to risk revealing your true self
To place your ideas and dreams before a crowd is to risk their loss
To love is to risk rejection
To live is to risk dying
To hope is to risk despair
To try is to risk failure.

But risks must be taken
Because one of the greatest dangers in life
Is to risk nothing.

Those who risk nothing
Do nothing, achieve nothing and become nothing
They may avoid suffering and sorrow
But they cannot learn, feel, change, grow, love or even live
Chained by their uncertainties, they are slaves
They have forfeited their freedom.

Only a person who risks all that he cannot keep,
To gain that which he can never lose . . .
Is truly free.

(*Anonymous poem, adapted by Simon Reynolds*)

4

Don't Go Breaking My Heart

BAZ GASCOYNE

After leaving Bible college in 1985, I went to live and work in Sheffield. A friend of mine worked for the YMCA as their Christian Outreach worker, and as part of our course at college we had been to do a week of schools' work with him. At the end of the week he had asked me to consider working with him voluntarily following my course. So that is what I did. I lived at the YMCA, which was an education in itself, and worked in schools and helped with youth services, weekends and other events.

My mother is one of those ladies who will only contact me if I am in trouble or something has happened that I need to know about. One morning I was informed that there was a telephone call for me at the reception desk. I picked the phone up and the conversation went as follows:

'Hello.'

'Barrie, it's your mother.'

(Now you need to know no one calls me Barrie except my mother and that's usually only when I'm in trouble.)

'Hi Mam, how are you?'

'I've got some news for you. Your gran is dead, bye.'

That was it, the phone line was dead and so was my gran. All those classes my mother had been to on 'how to break bad news sensitively' at the hospital had really come into their own that morning!

I stood there feeling numb. Tears began flowing down my cheeks as I thought of the fact I would never see my gran again. One of the receptionists became aware of me just standing there crying, so she asked me if there was anything wrong. I felt like saying, 'Oh no, I often do this on a morning before I go and take a lesson.' She was genuinely interested, but I spurted out 'My gran has died' and went to my room.

I sat in my room distraught. The lady I lived with for many years and who had looked after me like a mother had gone and I had not had the chance to see her one final time. There were so many things I wanted to say to her, like thanks for being there and putting up with me and my moods and anger at times. I wanted to tell her I loved her. I knew she had loved me by the way she looked after me. We have never been good as a family at telling one another that we love each other. I sat there wishing I could have one more chance to tell her, but that was not going to happen.

Suddenly there was a knock on my door and as I opened it I saw my mate Steve standing there with two cups of tea. What would we do without tea at times of trouble? Steve sat with me as I prattled on about everything and nothing, and even in the silence it was good to know someone was there to empathise with me.

Three days later I got another phone call from my mother. She was probably ringing to give me the details of the funeral, I thought. How wrong I was! The call went like this:

'Barrie it's your mother.'

'Hi Mam.'

'I've got some more news for you.'

I thought, 'Not more bad news.' 'What?' I asked.

'Your gran, she's not dead.'

'What do you mean, she's not dead?'

'I made a mistake – it's her next-door neighbour, Olive, who's dead. Bye.'

Once again the line was dead. But this time Gran was alive and kicking and Olive was dead!

I could not believe what I was hearing – apparently someone had told my mother that my gran had died, and then she found out three days later she was alive. Where have we heard that story before?

I was running around the YMCA building crying and shouting, 'She's not dead, she's alive!' People were looking at me as if I was mad. When people heard the story they were pleased for me, but in hysterics over how my mother had informed me both times of the news.

I was ecstatic that my gran was alive and I would have the chance to see her again and tell her I love her. When you love someone, and you discover they have died, your emotions are pulled all over the place – even more so when you know that they have died without knowing Jesus personally.

My gran was brought up with ten other brothers and sisters in quite a religious family. When she discovered I had become a Christian, she said the following to me in quite a stern tone: 'That Christianity might be okay for you, but do not try to get me into it. I want nothing to do with it, so don't bother talking to me about it.'

I found out some time later that she had been put off Christianity by her parents who made the children read the Bible every Sunday afternoon. I think one of her brothers didn't help the cause either.

I loved my gran and I had been given another chance to pray for her salvation, but also talk to her personally about Jesus. All the years I lived with my gran and granddad I knew that I had taken them for granted and sometimes abused the love they showed me. My granddad had died in the seventies. He had a painful death due to cancer. I remember standing outside his bedroom door one night, listening to him crying out to God, 'Please take me as I cannot bear the pain any more.'

When you love someone you want the best for them. If they are not Christians, you are desperate for them to discover God's love. If you don't, I would suggest you don't love them enough.

In John's Gospel chapter 11 we see what real love is. Jesus has heard his close friend Lazarus has died and is quite calm about the whole situation. Eventually he is moved by the weeping of Mary and the Jews over Lazarus' death. In verse 33 we read: 'When Jesus saw her weeping, and the Jews who had come along with her also weeping, he was deeply moved in spirit and troubled.' In verse 35 we read the shortest verse in the Bible: 'Jesus wept.'

Why did he weep? Because he had compassion for the people and he loved Lazarus. This doesn't mean a few tears down the face and quickly wipe them away before anyone sees you showing some emotion! But he wept, probably making a scene but not bothered what people thought as he was deeply moved by what was going on.

Until we are willing to let God break our hearts . . . we will never reach out to people to share the good news of Jesus.

If this kind of compassion was to engulf each Christian man, young and old, in this country we would soon have a revival of people coming to know Christ. Until we are willing to let God break our hearts with his love and compassion for the people of this nation and others, we will never reach out to people to share the good news of Jesus. The other day I was shocked as I read about a young boy being murdered and torched to death, and also of an elderly man who lived locally being beaten to death. What shocked me was how unmoved by these stories I was. I just pushed it aside with some thought of how society is getting worse.

It is so easy to get consumed with our everyday commitment that we lose the rhythm of God's heartbeat for our neighbours, school, college, university friends, work colleagues, family, friends and the different people we see or come across daily. Why is this? Is it because we have lost the first love of God in our own lives? Is it because we are no longer concerned about people dying without knowing God personally for themselves? Have we given up sharing our faith because we have lost confidence in the gospel, the good news of Jesus? Or is it simply because our hearts have become hard to the hurting, needy people in our society and world?

I was encouraged some years ago to pray the following prayer:

'God, will you give me the heart of Jesus, so I will feel as he feels for people? Will you give me the eyes of Jesus, so I will see as he does for people? Will you give me the mind of Jesus, so that I will think as he does about people? Will you give me the mouth of Jesus, so I will speak as he does to people? Will you give me the ears of Jesus, so I will listen as he does to people.'

When I have said this prayer sincerely, I have been amazed at the outcome. My heart at times has become heavy with pain as I listen to or talk with people about what is going on in their lives. I have started to see people in a different light; not through my own eyes of judgement but through eyes that really feel love and acceptance towards them. I want to reach out and be there for them in whatever way God sees fit.

Living this way is exciting and rewarding: letting God get hold of you and take you on the great rollercoaster journey of fun, laughter and tears which we call life, rubbing shoulders with those he has put in your path to make a difference in their lives and even introduce them to this living God. It's far better than allowing your heart to get hard and cold, becoming one of those people who just *used* to get excited about sharing their faith.

A few months after I had that really interesting phone call from my mother, I received another which went like this:

'Barrie, it's your mother. Your gran is in hospital; she is not very well.'

'What's wrong with her, Mam?'

'She's in a coma.'

'Are you sure?'

'Yes, I saw her today. She's in ward B4. Bye.'

Fortunately after the first phone call fiasco from my mother, I had been to Darlington a few times to visit my gran. So even though I was upset by the news, I had had the chance to see her. I phoned the hospital to see if I could arrange a time with them to see my gran outside visiting time. The reason for this was to avoid bumping into my father. He was my biological father – and that was it. He had lived in another country most of my life, and hated the sight of me – especially since I had become a Christian, probably because of some of the things he was involved with.

The hospital agreed to allow me some time in the evening after visiting hours to see my gran. I got the train up to Darlington and went to see my mother and brother in the daytime. In the evening I walked to the hospital, feeling very apprehensive about what I was going to see. My mother had prewarned me that my gran had lost a lot of weight and was now blind.

Hospitals are not my favourite places, and I have been known to faint at just the smell when I walk through the main doors! When I worked for a Methodist church in Northern Ireland I had to do hospital visits, and numerous times came out ready to puke or faint.

I managed to pull myself together and get to the ward. The nurse informed me that Gran was asleep and I had 15 minutes. I approached the bed cautiously and fearfully. There she was asleep, like a skeleton, so helpless and lifeless. This was not the lady who had worked so hard running her own bakery shop, or the lady who used to make the most fantastic sausage stew or Christmas cake. The lady who had such a distinguished laugh was not laughing any more. My gran was an amazing woman with whom I lived for many years during my childhood and later teens. I sat quietly looking at her frail body, thinking what a wonderful woman she was, when all of a sudden she woke. 'Gran, How are you?'

'You bloody idiot, she's dying,' I thought. Then she called out, 'Who's that?'

'It's Barrie,' I replied.

What she said next still brings a smile to my face.

'Nick?'

'No, Barrie.'

'Joe?'

'No, Barrie.'

'Buck?'

'No, Barrie.'

'John?'

'No, Barrie.'

This went on for some time as she went through the list of her brothers, sons, grandchildren and finally got to me. I asked her if she had had many visitors. She informed me that she hadn't, while constantly calling me by other people's names (no doubt the names of the many people who *had* visited her!).

What I was to hear next caused me to ask my gran to repeat what she had just said.

'I have had this man at the end of my bed who just kept saying to me, "Sarah, come to me I love you." He stands there with his arms open wide smiling at me urging me to come with him. Do you know who he could be?'

By then I was crying uncontrollably.

'It's Jesus, Gran,'

'What does he want with me?' she replied.

'He wants you to be with him.'

I went on to explain the gospel to my gran and told her how she could have assurance of eternal life before she died. She said she was going to pray and ask God to forgive her and ask Christ into her life. Immediately after that she stopped talking. Initially I thought she had died, so I lent over and listened. I could hear the faintest of breathing. I held her hand and prayed for her and then lent over and kissed her goodbye. I knew I would not see her again this side of eternity.

I left the hospital very emotional but grateful to God for that last time with my gran and for what he had done in her life while she had been in hospital. God had heard my prayers for my gran, asking specifically to have an opportunity to share with her about Jesus, and he had come through big time!

I ran and danced around the hospital car park, thanking God and shouting at Satan – telling him he had lost another battle to the Outrageous Grace of God. Tears streamed down my face as I experienced a combination of joy and sadness, knowing my gran was about to begin a brand new life with Jesus at the end of her own.

At her funeral I listened to the local vicar as he informed the mourners of the change in this lady's life in the last three weeks. As I smiled within, he commented on my gran's desire to pray, have the Bible read to her and take communion with him. I knew one day I would see Sarah McIntyre again, as this was just the beginning of her life at the grand age of 89.

During my visits to different churches to speak, or participate in youth weekends, I come across many people who struggle with sharing their faith. The main struggle is with guilt; guilt of not doing it or failing at it.

I believe this is often due to the way people are being discipled about evangelism. If we could get over to people that God wants to use us in sharing our faith in a natural and relevant way (where we remain emotionally honest), we would see a dramatic shift in the way people behave when opportunities come their way.

One of the biggest obstacles for men in sharing their faith today, I believe, is all to do with identity. A visiting speaker (Ray Booth) who was doing a three-week series on the Fatherhood of God, said in one of our meetings: 'If you grasp your true identity in God, that you are a Prince, a Son of God, this will affect every other area of your life.'

He went on to say: 'As you allow your relationship with your heavenly Father to improve, your worship, prayer, Bible reading, witness, work and family life will all improve.'

We need to understand that if we can experience this in our hearts, it will transform our endeavours. As Christian men today we need to have our hearts broken by the Holy Spirit so we will weep like Jesus did. Why? Because we will then see people and treat them as God wants us to. No longer will we be immune to the horrendous things we witness on the news or read in the papers, but we will actually be provoked to do something!

It's about time we men became real men, unafraid of emotions and prepared to carry godly burdens rather than our worldly ones.

Such an experience might mean we will cry as never before or hurt with a pain in our hearts as never before. Good! It's about time we men became real men, unafraid of emotions and prepared to carry godly burdens rather than our worldly ones. This is how God feels daily for his people, his world. Isn't it about time we had more of this within the church, but more importantly outside it where it really counts? How's your heart today?

Questions

1. When was the last time your heart was really broken by God?
2. Is your identity placed in God your Father or in your reputation?
3. Do you want to have the heart of God for people?
4. Are you willing to let him break it, no matter what the cost?
5. On a scale of 1–10, how would you rate yourself in the whole area of compassion?
6. Are you really bothered that people are dying without Jesus? If not, why not?

TEARS

I met an 84-year-old guy called George at a family party and he talked to me about when he was in the army.

They used to do smoke drills. Without breathing apparatus, and in total darkness, they had to get into a small tunnel. The tunnel was then filled with smoke and they had to walk through while holding the man in front of them. If they touched their eyes at any point they were given reprimands and they would end up in the eye hospital for days. When they got out they were all streaming with tears and he said how his mates used to laugh at each other because they were all crying so much.

People didn't cry in those days, especially men, and certainly not in public. George said he never saw his dad cry.

- Did you ever see your dad cry?
- When was the last time you cried?
- Why?
- Do you cry in private?
- Have your children ever seen you cry?

5
Effing and Jeffing!

JUSTIN THOMAS

Language is a frequent source of contention for Christians, and the specific issue of swearing, although a seemingly inconsequential topic for many, has provoked heated discussion over its appropriateness for use by followers of Jesus. In this chapter I hope to probe beyond the issues of common decency and acceptable behaviour in the culture of Western middle-class Christianity and look at some of the root questions of language and its use.

Three areas will be evident: blasphemy, swearing and the emotional content of language. We will look at the use of language as a whole, what principles and values need to guide our conversation, and what the Bible has to teach us. Then I will try to put in place underlying principles to help us deal with the various issues of speech. For example, where do we draw the line in joke-telling? What about sarcasm and innuendo? What about gossip and our culture of almost incessant micky-taking?

Probably the most common Christian response to swearing and the use of foul language would be to accept that in general it is not good. We want our speech to be salt and light, and as such we try to avoid swearing, especially with the 'F' word. However, we are human beings and need to express shock, surprise or frustration, so we tend to use debased forms of swear words. For example, 'gosh' instead of 'God', and 'blummin heck' instead of 'bloody hell'. We can also find incredibly creative and diverse uses for some of the not so obvious derogatory words such as 'cods' and 'pants'.

This response, while providing the user with an appearance of saintliness, fails to tackle any of the real depths to which language penetrates our lives, culture and very identities as human beings. Language provides the framework for our relationships, mediates our understanding of culture and context, and even to some extent our relationship with Jesus as we read the Scriptures in English or whatever is our native language. The issue of swearing alone causes us to think of the power of words to bless or curse. To 'cuss' at someone means literally to curse them.

Swearing throws up the question of the meaning of words. A word that many believers and non-believers alike find offensive is the 'C' word, literally referring to part of a woman's anatomy, yet most of these same folk would have little or no complaint with the use of the word 'berk'. Berk, however, derives its origin from the cockney rhyming slang Berkley-Hunt – so it is the same word!

We also need to think about the emotions that are carried in words. If it is wrong to speak in anger, does it matter whether the word we use is a swear word or some nice alternative? There is so much at work when we open our mouths, and yet most of us (and I'll be first to put up my hand and confess) give little thought to the content of our speech.

What I would like to do then is look at what Jesus and the Bible have to say about the use of language. Hopefully from this we can find principles to shape our use of language, and then it is up to you to sort out the day-to-day details with Jesus and the Christian friends you are accountable to.

The Bible has so much to say on the use of language that it would be impossible to deal comprehensively with it all here. Instead I will try to pull out some key highlights, and you will have to get reading yourself to get an even fuller picture.

> But what comes out of the mouth proceeds from the heart, and this is what defiles. For out of the heart come evil intentions, murder, adultery, fornication, theft, false witness, slander. These are what defile a person, but to eat with unwashed hands does not defile. (Matthew 15:18–20 NRSV)

Jesus is quite clear throughout his teaching that what really counts is what is on a person's heart. From our heart stems all our behaviour, thoughts, attitudes and reactions. Jesus died in order to restore our relationship with God, and the result of this is that the Holy Spirit comes and dwells in us to transform us as we submit to him. 'I will put my law within them, and I will write it on their hearts; and I will be their God, and they shall be my people' (Jeremiah 31:33 NRSV).

There is nothing worse than hearing a seething mass of hate or anger sugar-coated in impeccable conversation

---

God looks at and deals with our hearts, out of which springs everything of consequence in our lives including our speech. Any sinful thing that comes out of our mouths will have been birthed in our hearts. What comes out of our mouths will be a reflection of our relationship with God. If our words are full of anger or are conveying negativity, as opposed to building one another up in love, we need to not only discipline our mouths but dig down to the root cause and sort it out. There is nothing worse than hearing a seething mass of hate or anger sugar-coated in impeccable conversation, and there is no other answer to underlying heart issues than to spend time in prayer, submitting those things to Jesus on a daily basis.

In following on from Jesus' teaching, we can also see to some extent that it is not the words that we use that are sinful, so much as the emotional content and intent with which they are said. I only dare go so far as 'to some extent' because I think that there are perhaps some words that have their roots in sin, hate or oppression, and as such, while they might not carry sinful emotions of our own, we cannot divorce them from the sinful nature of their history. I believe that this is especially true with words that are rooted in racism, but there are other words, some of the sexual swear words for instance, whose roots are in abuse and therefore sin.

> For all of us make many mistakes. Anyone who makes no mistakes in speaking is perfect, able to keep the whole body in check with a bridle . . . but no one can tame the tongue – a restless evil, full of deadly poison. With it we bless the Lord and Father, and with it we curse those who are made in the likeness of God. From the same mouth come blessing and cursing. My brothers and sisters, this ought not to be so. (James 3:2; 8–10 NRSV)

James cuts right to the chase in his letter. We are sinful, imperfect and inconsistent people. Blessings and curses flow far too easily from our mouths with the same breath. Our mouths, that express love to God, need to be consistent in expressing love to our neighbour.

> Those who say, 'I love God', and hate their brothers or sisters, are liars; for those who do not love a brother or sister whom they have seen, cannot love God whom they have not seen. (1 John 4:20 NRSV)

> But I say to you, Do not swear at all, either by heaven, for it is the throne of God, or by the earth, for it is his footstool, or by Jerusalem, for it is the city of the great King. And do not swear by your head, for you cannot make one hair black or white. Let your word be 'Yes, Yes' or 'No, No'; anything more than this comes from the evil one. (Matthew 5:34–37 NRSV)

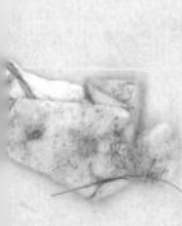

This command of Jesus is not entirely dissimilar to James' comments. A person only needs to take an oath when there is doubt over the truthfulness of their normal speech. Jesus' command is that all our speech be truthful and reliable to the extent that we should never need to swear by anything. He also points out the futility of such oaths due to their inability to make a difference to anything important. Jesus stresses the need for consistency in the integrity of our speech.

> Whatever house you enter, first say, 'Peace to this house!' And if anyone is there who shares in peace, your peace will rest on that person; but if not, it will return to you. (Luke 10:5–6 NRSV)

This teaching was given by Jesus to the 72 disciples he sent out to the towns and places he intended them to visit. We catch a glimpse here of the power that words can have for

We live in a culture that values words very cheaply.

good. Jesus does not tell his disciples to pray for peace for the house but to speak it out. They are acting in the name of Jesus and their words carry the power of the authority that Jesus gave them. We live in a culture that values words very cheaply and yet there is a great deal of power in the use of words for good or ill. Many of us will have grown up with the childhood phrase 'Sticks and stones may break my bones but names will never hurt me', and all of us will know how wrong that saying is. If you're talking long-term damage to people, then names and cursing words do the real damage. A careless, throwaway sentence can, and frequently does, cripple people for years; the implications of which can be felt for generations without some kind of healing taking place.

> And let us consider how to provoke one another to love and good deeds, not neglecting to meet together, as is the habit of some, but encouraging one another, and all the more as you see the Day approaching. (Hebrews 10:24–25 NRSV)

In the light of the last passage we can see how significant this teaching is. As we recognise the power of words to harm, we begin to see the opposite is true: there is power that we can unleash through encouragement. Indeed we know we have an enemy whose name is the 'father of lies' and who is more than eager to spread hurt and dismay through oppressive words. Though we can come on our own in prayer to find healing for our hurts in Jesus, the power to overcome is found in encouraging one another. This is because as we find ourselves coming under the weight of negative words spoken about us, we do not have the confidence or the belief in our relationship with God to accept the truth God is saying to us. We need to be persistent and enthusiastic in building one another up in love in order that we are fully able to take the blessing we have received and make it known to the world.

Hebrews 10 also teaches that we should encourage each other 'all the more as you see the Day approaching'. The day in question is the day of Jesus' return. The only real sign we have from Scripture of that day's approach is that every tribe and people group will have been reached by the good news of Jesus. This means that the more successful our evangelism is, the more we need to encourage one another. Surely it would make sense to need more encouragement when we are not doing well, but the truth is the more successful we are, the more opposition, lies and attack we will face from the enemy. We must not hold back out of pride or jealousy, but humbly push one another on.

> But be filled with the Spirit, as you sing psalms and hymns and spiritual songs among yourselves, singing and making melody to the Lord in your hearts, giving thanks to God the Father at all times and for everything in the name of our Lord Jesus Christ. (Ephesians 5:18–20 NRSV)

Sounds freaky, I know, but it makes sense! Our hearts and therefore our speech should be full of thanks and praise to God. And the 'among yourselves' bit pushes home the encouragement factor when we talk about God and worship him together. I was privileged in the autumn of

2000 to go with a team to Wales for a week to pray. There were half a dozen of us and it was the first time I had gone away for a week solely with the intent to pray for the place we were going to. There was no other agenda than to bless in prayer another part of the nation. As a result we were pretty focused, and there was always someone there who would pray aloud or even just repeat the name of Jesus or a sentence of worship. The result was an almost continual atmosphere of prayer and one of the most intense periods of intimacy and closeness with God I have known. I realise that this type of experience isn't very sustainable in the context of having to go to work where I am not surrounded by other believers, yet I caught a glimpse of the power of spurring one another on in praise of Jesus. 'Let your speech always be gracious, seasoned with salt, so that you may know how you ought to answer everyone' (Colossians 4:6).

Our speech needs to be full of grace, for we are forbidden to judge others. We also need to be quite deliberate in seasoning our speech with the salt. I am certainly guilty of hurting others, especially those close to me, through careless words. The opposite of this is to speak love and encouragement through careful words. Words that are full of care have a power to open up situations and conversations and allow Jesus into them. As we bring a measure of care to what we say, we take time to think. This thinking space gives us time to hear from the Holy Spirit; hence we know what to say.

'You shall not make wrongful use of the name of the Lord your God, for the Lord will not acquit anyone who misuses his name' (Exodus 19:9). Blasphemy is one area God is pretty clear on and the only possible loophole you could argue for is that the name of the Lord refers to the name Yahweh specifically and not the more general name

'God'. But let's face it, if you're looking for loopholes then your best bet is to ask a Christian mate if they can come round, and when they do get them to give you a kick up the backside, figuratively speaking, of course . . .

I believe that these passages from the Bible give us a well-rounded set of principles by which we need to try and shape our use of language. The only problem is that by pulling out all these Scripture soundbites, we are in danger of creating an ideal that will cause us never to speak again for fear of saying the wrong thing. We live under grace not law. The passage we looked at from James says it straight. All of us make many mistakes, and he makes this fact clear before he speaks about perfection. We know we will never achieve perfection this side of heaven, yet a way has been opened for us through Jesus to enable us to enter heaven. Our means of moving towards this perfection and of finding the grace and forgiveness for our failings lies in our faith in him.

Jesus taught his disciples to pray 'Give us this day our daily bread' (Matthew 6:11). Jesus taught us to ask God our Father to meet our needs. We can only ask this on a daily basis; tomorrow we must come and ask again. Why? Because just as the Israelites received the manna in the desert on a daily basis, and any they tried to keep until the day after went mouldy overnight, so we need to come to God daily in order that our faith and relationship with God stays living and active. It is also more important, I believe, to focus on the positive aspects of speech, such as encouraging others, rather than concentrating on the negatives, such as stopping swearing. Love covers over a multitude of sins. Indeed as we ask for our daily bread we must remember that Jesus said 'My food is to do the will of him who sent me and to complete his work' (John 4:34).

Our spiritual nourishment and fullness comes from doing the will of God. I confess that I am still prone to swear more than occasionally, yet the challenge I have felt from my time spent in prayer has been to strive to be more of an encourager and to become more loving in my speech. A consequence of this has been that the frequency with which expletives come out of my mouth has decreased, but more important to me has been the way my relationships have grown through simple affirmation and encouragement. The strength for this has been a direct result of an increase of time in prayer with Jesus. I am absolutely convinced that this is the bottom line with all our discipleship issues: spending time with our Saviour. There is no other source from which we can draw the power we need to break out in a culture that is so oppressive when it comes to the use and abuse of language.

Questions

1. Can you swear without using a rude word?
2. Do you swear in public? Or in the car on your own?
3. Does it matter if you 'think' a swear word but don't speak it?
4. How can we help each other in our use of speech?
5. How can you use your speech to encourage others?

6
Fantasy Island

BAZ GASCOYNE

In the 1980s there was a TV programme called *Fantasy Island*. Each week people from all walks of life would fly to an exotic island and have their fantasies fulfilled. The owner of the island was like a modern version of Father Christmas or an American version of *Jim'll Fix It*. He would be informed of the arrival of these people by his faithful colleague, Tattoo, who would go running to him, shouting as he pointed to the sky, 'Boss, Boss, de plane.'

People's fantasies varied from meeting a long lost love or doing something for the last time before they died, to having the chance to relive a day and rectify a mistake or regret. Each week you knew people were going to leave the island satisfied as they had fulfilled their fantasy.

If it were that easy to have our fantasies fulfilled a lot more men would get themselves into trouble and mess up their lives and other people's. William A. Orton once said, 'If you keep your mind sufficiently open, people will throw a lot of rubbish into it.' How true this is. Each day we are bombarded with information by the media, which if we are not careful can have us sliding down the hill of fantasy and lustful desires.

Unfortunately, as a young boy, I got into masturbation far too early. I say 'unfortunately' not because masturbation in itself is wrong, but because it got me opening my mind to all sorts of fantasy.

It all started when I was about ten years old. One day, as I met some friends in the local fields to play, I was presented with the question, 'Have you had your first wank yet?' I had no idea what they were on about, which they probably knew by the look of puzzlement on my face. So they took me into some bushes and showed me what they meant. After they had done it to themselves they informed me it was my turn. I felt scared and embarrassed and did not want to continue this sex education lesson. However, it was made very clear to me that if I didn't I could no longer be part of their gang – they were about five years older than me and I loved knocking around with them.

When I got home I felt very confused. I was excited by the sensation I had just experienced, but the circumstances in which it had happened made me feel angry, upset and full of hatred.

I did, however, continue to masturbate at home in the luxury and privacy of my bedroom. I was determined to become a man. I was going for the world record. If there had been an event at the Olympics I certainly would have represented Great Britain and probably won the gold medal!

I tell you this not to shock or embarrass anyone but to show that most men get into this through discovery with their peers rather than their parents; which, for a lot of men when they later become Christians, creates feelings of embarrassment, guilt and dirtiness.

As a teenager you knew you were not the only person masturbating. Most of us have gone through the phase of fantasising about the latest sexy TV or film star, or the girl at school we fancied, or our mate's mother or our schoolteacher. I can relate to Jonathan Ross when he said to Britt Eckland in last year's Comedy Awards, 'Can I thank you for helping me to get through my difficult years.'

At the age of 17, when I became a Christian, I was still trying to get into the *Guinness Book of Records*. Gradually, through prayer, reading the Bible, attending church and being involved with other Christians, God began to make me aware of sin in my life: stealing, jealousy, hatred, anger, lust, and numerous other things. I started to become aware that sin was messing up the person God wanted me to be, as well as my relationship with him.

In the Christian world there are different views on the subject of masturbation. Some people will tell you it is a sin, and others will tell you to put it under the cold tap, or that you need to be more disciplined. Usually none of these men own up to the fact that they once struggled or are still struggling with it.

Before Linda and I were married, we were at church together one day, and she was leading worship while I was there as part of the congregation. At the end of the meeting an opportunity was given for people to receive prayer. Quite a lot of people responded to this. One of the leaders of the church asked if I would pray for a young man in the worship team who had acknowledged he would like prayer. So I went up to this guy and offered to pray for him. After about five minutes' silence he plucked up enough courage to inform me what he wanted prayer for. Yes, you've guessed it: masturbation. I now knew I had a decision to make – to pretend to be holy and nod my head in a holy way, or be honest and tell him I was struggling as well. I chose the latter and said to him, 'Great, you pray for me and I'll pray for you.' Before we even began, you could see that he was already feeling better. Was this down to the fact he didn't feel judged or condemned, and someone knew the struggles he was going through?

In the 1980s a well-known church leader, speaker and author offended a lot of other Christian leaders by his remarks on masturbation. He said something like: 'It's not a sin to masturbate, but I have not met anyone who does not sin while masturbating.' What he was implying was that to get aroused you have to let your mind enter fantasy island, which then leads to sin. Because of this, some Christian leaders refused to be on the same platform as him, even though most of them would have done exactly what this man implied at some time in their lives and probably as Christians.

Masturbation can and does become habitual in any man's life if he keeps feeding his sexual fantasies. Woody Allan said in the film *Annie Hall* (1977), 'Don't knock masturbation. It's sex with someone I love.' This is very funny, but it's not true! Yes, you may love your willy, but with you and your willy are the sordid thoughts to accompany the act of masturbation!

We do not read in the Bible 'Thou shalt not masturbate', so what is God's view? Does this mean it's not an issue with him or that it's OK to do it? I read a Christian magazine recently whose entire edition was dedicated to exploring the issue of sex. There was a section entitled 'Should we scratch the itch?'

> So where does masturbation fit into the arena? Many people both single and married find sexual release in this practice.
>
> When you have no partner, your sex drive still goes on. But it's vital to manage it correctly – whether you're married or not. Just like physical hunger, your sex drive needs the right nutrition – not junk food like pornography or fantasies.
>
> So if you are married: wish your partner were with you. If you are single: 'scratch the itch'. But be careful of over indulgence.
>
> We do need to be able to discuss the issue of masturbation. In the past we have been either silent and embarrassed, or heavy and condemning. There is no actual teaching in the Bible on masturbation, but there are clear directives concerning other sexual practices.
>
> Concerning masturbation it would seem that God leaves it to the individual to decide what's right for him or her. (*Compass*, Vol. 1, No. 3)

This was a very interesting and challenging article, which surely raised some eyebrows, and no doubt will cause a few feathers to be stirred even now as you read it!

I am not knocking masturbation for the sake of it, but I am challenging the way we allow our minds to be filled with things that are not conducive to our Christian walk or our future lives, whether we plan to be single or married. If we plan to marry in the future, or if we are already married, the enemy will try and use the things we store up in our minds to bring division between ourselves and our partner.

When I was a young teenager of about 16 I had one fantasy that ruled my thought life nearly every day. This was to be seduced by an older lady. The reason for this was that I thought that if I could sleep with an older woman she would be able to teach me how to make love to women in a way that I would not feel a novice. On two occasions I have had women older than me make a pass at me, the first when I was 16 working as an apprentice central heating engineer. The lady whose house we were working in started to come on to me. Even though I had dreamt about such a thing happening, when it did I became Norman Wisdom personified. With a very high-pitched voice I started to call for my boss who was working upstairs!

The second time this happened was years later at a Christian meeting I had been speaking at. After the meeting had finished, food and drinks were provided in another room. Before I knew what was happening this lady made a pass at me. I must admit, part of me was enjoying it as it was doing wonders for my ego. However, I knew I had to get out of the situation, so I suggested we went and joined the others. As I left the house to drive back home I passed this lady at the bus stop. It was pouring down with rain, and I had two voices speaking to me. One was saying, 'Pull over and give her a lift home,' the other was saying, 'Keep driving. Don't stop.' You will be pleased to hear I chose to listen to the latter. I drove back to Sheffield breaking the speed limit. I went straight to my friend's house, got him out of bed and asked him to pray for me.

Paul knew what he was talking about when he said, 'Flee from your youthful desires' (2 Timothy 2:22). In *The Message* it reads, 'Run away from infantile indulgence.' Three days later I received a letter from this lady asking me if we could meet up. She also informed me that she had been having an affair with her minister. So once again I went to see my friend, and this time showed him the letter. He prayed for me and we destroyed it.

Unfortunately, like most young men, I mixed up the difference between lust and love. Desperate for love and intimacy, I pursued my lustful desires and became addicted to masturbation and the world of fantasy.

As we know, Satan is a slimy beggar. He knows the weak areas in our lives, and that's where he aims his lies and accusations. In 2 Corinthians 10:5 it says, 'We take captive every thought to make it obedient to Christ.'

A couple of years ago a film came out entitled *American Pie*. This was a comedy about four young men and their pursuit to lose their virginity at their graduation party. There is one clip in it where the mother of one of the guys makes a pass at one of these young men. As soon as I saw this part of the film it triggered all my emotions and thoughts of the past and my fantasy with older women. I knew I would have to make an agreement with my wife, friends and myself not to watch that film again. Ephesians 4:27 says, 'And do not give the devil a foothold.' This is what I am trying to do now. I cannot say I always succeed, but I am getting better.

So in conclusion I want to ask you to be honest with yourself, God and your friends when you work through the questions.

Questions

1. What fantasies are you still struggling with?
2. Can you masturbate without fantasising?
3. Should we 'scratch the itch'?
4. Is it OK for a married man to masturbate?
5. Do you stay up late watching films you know are not helpful for you to be watching?

6. Are you taking captive your thoughts, or are they taking you captive?
7. Do you need to make yourself accountable to someone with the things you read, watch, log onto on your computer or fantasise about?
8. If Jesus was tempted in every way, as we are, yet was without sin (Hebrews 4:15) was he ever tempted by sex? What do you think?
9. Is your life ruled by love or lust?
10. Do you have control over your fantasies or do they have control over you?

BOSSES

Why are most bosses still men in this new millennium? Do we arrange our structures in business and church to keep women down? Be honest in your discussions.

Why is it seen as acceptable to have half-naked women in national newspapers every day?

7

Finding the Answer

Tim Hewitt

What would life be like if we knew all the answers? What would a birthday be without surprises? Why do we try to put God in a box so that we can understand him? And then when we think we do, get bored with him? Because if you know all the answers you don't need questions, and that's why God is hiding, waiting to be found.

I used to do assemblies in a Church of England primary school. I loved it because the kids were so close to the kingdom of heaven and taught me loads about Jesus. But there was one thing that used to upset me and make me angry. Every question I asked, would produce the same three replies: God, Jesus or the Holy Spirit. 'Why did Jesus die?' *'God.'* What is Easter about? *'The Holy Spirit.'* How did God make the world?' *'Jesus.'* They had been taught that the right answer for everything was Jesus, God or the Holy Spirit. A profound truth in one way, but the very thing that could lead them to Jesus, their inquisitiveness, had been destroyed.

I'm just the same. I still sit in church and hear sermon

after sermon giving me the answers that I already know, so I don't bother asking questions. Once again I've lost out on discovering God. God isn't in the answers I think I know; he's in the journey of discovery, waiting to surprise me.

God is the same yesterday, today and for ever, but you can still discover more of him, journey further into his depths and be amazed. If you don't ask questions, you'll believe lies. Truth gets twisted in your head and God becomes something he's not. You lose the child inside that asks why.

The answers become less important when you ask the right questions. Knowing the answer doesn't bring a sense of peace; it's the path of discovery that leads to seeing more of yourself in Jesus and knowing that he loves you. Jesus is bigger than your understanding, more wild than your imagination, more reckless than the box you first put him in, more vast than your dreams and more loving than you can handle. When Jesus has found you along the way, you have found truth, and the only response is to surrender.

Truth is always an experience and never just a body of knowledge. That's why God can shame the wise with the foolish things of this world. A little kid can teach you more about Jesus, and knowing all the right answers can kill your spirit. I don't only want to know *about* Jesus, I want to know him.

For ages I have been using all the 'right' answers to help me get over my problems; to leapfrog them as if they weren't there, and get on with my life. So why do I carry so much baggage and hold on to past hurts? Jesus doesn't want us to get over our problems; he wants us to walk through them with him: 'Even though I walk through the valley of the shadow of death, I will fear no evil' (Psalm 23:4).

We need to be real and authentic in our faith, even if the answers make us ask more questions. This kind of authentic faith and real Christianity is the kind my friends can relate to. They have problems; I have problems. If I'm walking through my problems with Jesus, suddenly there is something of themselves mirrored in what I'm doing and being. They see the pain, the hurt, the uncertainty and doubt, but also the bright shining amazing grace of hope they've been searching for. Jesus loves the mess we bring to him. It wasn't the sinners, prostitutes or tax collectors that Jesus had a problem with, it was the Pharisees who thought they had all the right answers.

In the film *The Matrix*, Neo is given a pill to disrupt his systems, so he can wake up to the way things really are. Many people are happy to drift along being lost, then when a crisis comes their way they suddenly wake up, start asking questions and find Jesus. It is our job to share our questions with each other and those who don't know Jesus. This is discipleship; welcoming strangers not only into our homes but also into our stories. Sharing means listening, not just waiting your turn to speak. What questions do others have? Let them challenge you. At the junction where our questions and stories connect, they may find Jesus. Point him out; he'll make sense of their story. He's the big story in which our little story is found. Jesus preached using questions and stories about people to show heavenly truth. He rarely gave answers unless he was asked for them, and then he answered with more questions!

In this confused, noisy, fast-paced world, let's dare to say, 'I don't know.' Let's dare to doubt; dare to be honest with God.

OPENNESS AND HONESTY

We need to learn to relate to one another – without pretence – so we can be the body that God is calling us to be and spur one another on to love and good deeds! We need one another! Reality – we're sinners. We mess up! We're on the same side. We need to watch one another's back and keep each other red hot and holy! We need to love one another – *truly* love one another! (Caleb)

I wish someone had told me it's all right to cry. I also wish that there was a simple creed for men. Not like the doctrine creeds we have in our services, more like a simple statement of what our relationships are to be based on. What does our faith mean for relationships with God, wife and family? What does it mean for workplace, community and conflict? We need a commonsense Christianity as well as the new emphases that sweep the church every few years. (Dave)

8
Global Village
Greg Valerio

Does the global village exist? It does to me! As I drive down Route 66 post twin towers holocaust, seen live on TV in some sick repeat of our worst nightmare, I watch the smoke stacks holding their breath as if in anticipation of the impending energy crisis on the west coast of America. Past Los Alamos Nuclear Power and Research Plant, paranoid over the threat of terrorist attacks. Through Tulsa (that boasts to me of the huge steak served blue from the prairies of the Mid West). I listen to the 'Savage Nation' proselytising Israeli propaganda on the thousand-year Jihad against Christianity and the lifestyle of the West. This seems no different from Jerry Falwell and Pat Robertson who were reported to have blamed 11th September on the moral decline of the USA brought about by gay and lesbian people.

I fight back the psychological outrage of the global communication networks that feed me information faster than I can process. I wage war on myself because I am impotent to change the rising tide of war, revenge and the fatalism that wells within me. It's not that I rage against the machine and its technologically advanced mechanics; I war with myself, my spirituality, my God and the apparent hopelessness that an ever-expanding world thrusts upon me. I am grateful for the information; grateful for the internet, grateful for the access it gives me to information and the vast array of cultural perspectives I can feed myself with at the touch of a button. Yet this very gratitude is like the beetle that's eating away at the Elm tree. In time it will topple the faith we place in the immediate culture we have created.

This justice demands more than the evangelical preoccupation with 'saving souls' or 'new models of church that will (finally!) facilitate revival'.

I once heard a man talk about watching a child shit itself to death; he was left with no other words than 'the shame, the shame, the shame'. The global village is to some a defining reality, to others a dream of what we can become, to others a nightmare. It is morally irreconcilable that in monetary terms 'the growth in global advertising now outpaces the growth in the world economy by one-third'.[1] If I am tortured by the world I live in, then I deserve to be when millions of children die of diarrhoea every year because of my cultural selfishness.

Christianity is a faith of action; action that is rooted in the justice of God. This justice demands more than the evangelical preoccupation with 'saving souls' or 'new models of church that will (finally!) facilitate revival'. This justice requires a spirituality that transcends the personal

[1] 1998 United Nations Human Development Report.

preoccupation we all have with what we do with our genitals, or the male ghost of masturbation (I understand that women suffer from this demon too). If the totality of my faith is to listen to anointed preachers tell me from the platform about how we are going to save the world, I think I may become a Jesus-centred Buddhist. The day of the platform preacher is over, or should be; the day of the self-styled guru (so-called 'anointed') man of God is over, or should be; the day of the charismatic prophet who quivers when delivering a piece of inspired intuition must stop. Christian spirituality, if reduced to this level of soap-opera popular culture, no longer enshrines the values or the heartbeat of God. And these are the values that must become ours too.

God's justice is not a demand or a social ethic; it is not an extra or a central part of the life of the body of Christ. It *is* the body of Christ. How I live and behave as a Christian must be defined by the priorities of the gospel. God's justice is a reflection of his personality. Father, Son and Holy Spirit live together as Three in One and One in Three. We worship (and should reflect in our relationships with one another and the world) a trinitarian God who is perfect relationship, perfect love, perfect communication, and whose will is enshrined in action as well as words.

By enshrining these values into our lives, we build a community that is genuinely countercultural.

As we reflect upon the trinity we are inspired to meditate upon the world and identify where our society no longer reflects that perfect relationship. Jesus, the incarnation of a trinitarian God, encapsulated this idea in the teaching on the Sermon on the Mount. The poor, the grieving, the humble, the merciful, the justice seekers, the pure of heart and purpose, the persecuted, the misunderstood, the peacemakers all become the ideal and object of our life's work. By enshrining these values into our lives, we build a community that is genuinely countercultural. We reflect a gospel that no longer apes popular culture because of its morally impotent message and desperation to be heard, but begins to redefine culture for the benefit of the poor, the marginalised and the dispossessed. This justice, this lifestyle, this radicalism becomes the aroma of Christ to our world and the cause to which people are willing to give their lives.

I am willing to give my life for the dignity of the homeless because it is righteous and just.

I am willing to shop as ethically as I can because it invests worth in the labour of those that produce my food.

I am willing to campaign to change the terms of trade between rich and poor countries because the increasing gap between rich and poor is morally unjustifiable.

I am willing to limit my lifestyle because resources spent on the expansion of my middle-class lifestyle are resources diverted away from the greater needs of the poor.

Our lives are the true reflection of what we believe, and our actions as Christians in the global village must be tangible and just. I can wrap up my faith in Christ in the trappings and trimmings of popularity but, in my experience, those that are attracted to Jesus through these means, whether in the UK or Tanzania, ultimately see through the shallow nature of cultural relevance and demand something more substantial.

Lifestyle is the key to engaging the global village. It is true that we are all participants in this village. We are all aware of the implications for us and those we are never likely to meet. As I parade my new Gap top, Nike shoes, eat my mass-farmed breakfast cereal, climb into my German car, buy my child the latest Mickey Mouse Disney toy, I eat at the table of what we call the global free market; the market where items are manufactured or grown in one part of the world and bought and consumed in another.

An example of this would be the manufacture of Nike Athletic Shoes. These are produced in many Export Processing Zones (EPZ). 'These are tax-free havens where goods are mass-produced in sweatshop conditions. One factory in China (the Wellco factory) pays workers $0.16 per hour, and runs 11–12 hour shifts, 7 days a week. Workers are fined if they refuse to work overtime, overtime rates are not paid, most employees have no legal contract, corporal punishment has been reported, workers are fined if they are caught talking, approximately ten children were found in the sewing section and virtually no employee had heard of the Nike Code of Conduct'.[2]

This situation is not new, not uncommon and can be found virtually anywhere in the world in any industry. It is one example of how we are linked to the global world through global trade and consumption and have a global responsibility to act as righteously as we can. It is here that a justice-orientated lifestyle kicks in.

Begin the journey

We begin by asking what do we believe in? By that I don't mean just Jesus: if we say we believe in Jesus and change

[2] Naomi Klein, *No Logo*, Table 9.3 p.474 (Flamingo 2000)

nothing in our lives, other than our personal morality, we are hypocrites and have missed the point of following Christ. But we ask ourselves, what did Jesus believe in? Jesus believed in justice, righteousness and compassion for the poor. He believed in challenging unjust structures that perpetuated violence and poverty and he attacked the roots of the problem in human selfishness and greed. Therefore if we say we follow Christ, so we must do as he did.

We then move on to how our lifestyle needs to change in order to reflect the values of Jesus. Perhaps we need to recycle paper as a way of not wasting resources, or shop more ethically by buying Café Direct fair trade coffee, or Green & Blacks organic chocolate, or researching if there is an organic producer who delivers to the door. By doing these things, we are not only expressing a concern for our environment, but we are giving tangible expression to what we believe in.

We can then begin to look into getting involved with groups or networks that are actively working on issues relating to the poor, the marginalised and the dispossessed. We could join in a campaign that is working to see the trade rules around the world made fairer for poor countries. We could support a work among prostitutes in our own country or overseas. Or perhaps, if you are feeling really revolutionary, write to a company and complain about their practices and say you will be telling all your friends what they are up to and you will not buy their product. At this time action speaks louder than words and Christians must be at the forefront of seeing the world changed into a fairer and more just society for all people.

This is not an exhaustive list of things that can be done, but they represent some of the things that my household has done over the last five years. It must be recognised that this is a journey that you embark upon at some cost to yourself. You will discover just how little you know about the world; just how unjust our society is and how we are all complicit in the oppression of the poor. You will discover your own likes and dislikes, your prejudices and bigotry and, I dare say, a little cultural racism and superiority as well. This is a journey for the strong, the courageous and the dedicated; it is not a journey for the closed-minded, the cultural supremacist and egocentric among us.

I have not had the opportunity in this short space to talk in more detail about the lives of the poor, the fact that the global village means global misery to millions and that preaching at people in the form of crusades and evangelistic meetings leaves a bitter taste in the mouths of many and does little more than create 'rice' Christians and boost statistics. Or that the internet revolution is only a revolution if you have electricity, literacy and the money to buy a computer. (As I found recently in Ethiopia, when discussing a Human Rights situation with community leaders from the slums, my technological sophistication was clearly beyond their capability of participation.) In a society that has reduced Christianity to a mere personal choice and moral framework, we need the strong and courageous to put substance back into what it means to follow Christ. Our lives must demonstrate the substance of the gospel and the justice of God.

It is my personal conviction that as we enter the twenty-first century, the work of the Spirit of Christ in the world will focus more on issues of peace, justice and reconciliation than ever before. The global village gives us global access, and with global access we carry an ever greater responsibility to act and behave in such a way as to honour Christ in thought, word and deed.

Greg Valerio is Director of Cred (Christian, Relief, Education & Development). For more information on the work of Cred contact greg@cred.org.uk or write to Cred, P.O. Box 63, Chichester PO19 2FE.

LIFE RULES

1. Learn about yourself from your reactions more than from your actions.
2. Own your ruling passions – good and bad – because you can only disown the negative ones once you have owned them!
3. As quickly as possible get into team contexts that include working with women, and learn to free your emotions and get in touch with your feminine side.
4. Establish a lifestyle with clear expectations of openness, honesty, accountability and vulnerability.

(Pete)

9
Hide and Seek

Baz Gascoyne

At the age of seventeen-and-a-half I became a Christian. Six months prior to that I was on the brink of death.

I took a cocktail of alcohol and tablets. I did not want to die; it was just a cry for help and attention. While in hospital, after having my stomach pumped and numerous blood tests, I had three days of lying around thinking. Questions were rushing through my mind such as 'What if I die?' 'Where would I go?' 'Is there a heaven or a hell?' I had no answers to these questions and neither did anyone else I knew.

I discharged myself from hospital and tried to get on with my life as if nothing had happened. Unfortunately, for the next six months, I went through a phase of depression. Up to that point I thought depression was when the alarm would go off to get up for work. Now I found I would be in a pub with my mates, and if somebody started laughing I thought they were laughing at me. At work I would be helping to put a central heating system in when I would just start crying, not because I had flooded the house, but because something was going on deep inside my mind and heart. I refused to go and see the psychiatrist because of the fear of my mates finding out. I didn't want them to think I was going mad.

Six months later I went for a week's holiday with some of my friends who were involved with a youth club. The place we had gone to was Cliff College, which is based in the Peak District. Hundreds of other young people were there from all around the UK. This was an annual event called the Derwent Week. Most, if not all, of the young people were Christians. My friends and I decided that we would visit the local pub every night and get hammered. The main reason for me being there was to get drunk, try and 'get off' with a girl, but more importantly just to get away from home and escape from what was going on in my life.

Every morning I would go along to one of the smaller meetings. I decided to go to one because I liked the look of a girl in the group from Bath. There were about 30 people in the group, all of a similar age. Each day we would look at some aspect of the Christian faith and the Bible, and each day the guy who was leading the group, Peter, would ask me for my opinion. So I would give a load of abusive language about why I didn't believe in this stuff. I was trying really hard to upset and embarrass him. Every time he would thank me for my contribution and move on, never looking flustered or shocked by what I had just said.

I was there only because of this girl and because the pub wasn't open. However, God had me there for other reasons. Each day we would go through the same process: Peter asking me to share and then the room turning blue and him replying 'thanks for that Baz'. Every time I would start to rant, some of the group started to read their Bibles (yeah right!), due to their embarrassment of what was going on, but Peter just accepted me for who I was.

After five mornings together, Peter suggested that we made or bought a small present for the person we had been sitting next to all week. Yes, you guessed it . . . I was sat next to this girl. So I bought her a lovely white pocket-sized Bible and said something complimentary about her. I had

I had been kidding myself, thinking that my life was full when in fact it was desperately empty.

been sitting next to Peter and couldn't wait to see what he had bought me. Everyone else had given their presents to each other. I was the last one. Peter began by saying how much he had enjoyed the week, and how much he had appreciated my input. He went on to say, 'I've not bought Baz anything.' I thought, 'Great! I have spent pounds on that girl and he's not got me a thing. That's typical of a minister, the stingy beggar.' He went on to say, 'I've written Baz a letter I want him to read later.' 'A letter! I can't believe I'm hearing this,' I thought. He continued, 'I've also got him this.' He then pulled out of his pocket a rubber band. It was about six inches long and half-an-inch thick. I couldn't believe my eyes. He said that this represented my life at that moment, but if I let God into my life it could be 'like this' – he then stretched it to its full potential. As he did this something began to happen. I felt as if someone or something had punched me in the heart. I could feel all the anger and pain welling up inside. I wanted to shout, 'Will someone help me?' I got up from my chair, grabbed the letter and the rubber band and ran out of the room.

When I was by myself, I opened the letter (which I still have today), and read:

'Dear Baz,

It has been good to have you in the group this week. You have entered into everything very well, even when you were asked to share with me yesterday. I am going to comment on your enthusiasm when I say a word about you.

I don't know if you have made that decision to give yourself to the Lord Jesus Christ. I can only encourage you to do so if you have not. The Christian life is the most demanding and costly life, but certainly the most joyful and satisfying.

Trust that everything goes well for you in the immediate future and throughout your life.

Have a great day today.

Yours in His care,

Peter.

As I read the letter I knew that I had been kidding myself, thinking that my life was full when in fact it was desperately empty. The motivation of trying to be someone I wasn't was no longer helping. All day I kept thinking about Christianity and this guy called Jesus. Could it be possible that I could know God for myself like these young people said they knew him?

I arranged to see Peter before tea so I could talk to him privately about this Christianity. He explained to me about the good news of Jesus: why he died on the cross, the consequences of sin and how I could know God's forgiveness and his love. I knew deep down this was what I wanted. I asked him what I needed to do and he said simply pray.

I had a problem with this. The only model I had seen was the vicar at the church I visited for Boys' Brigade services. He would whistle when he talked at the end of certain words or sentences. His voice also seemed to go up an octave when he prayed. Did I need to do that? Peter told me to talk to God as I would talk to my best friend. OK, I thought, here goes.

'God, my life is a bloody mess. I don't need to be told that I have sinned; I know I have. I have hurt a lot of people by what I've done and what I've said to them and about them. Will you please forgive me for this and other sins I have done? You know the anger, hatred and pain in my life – will you please deal with this? Thank you that your Son died for all the shit in my life; please forgive me and help me to be the person that you want me to be. God, will you please help this not to be a fad that lasts a few months then fades away? Let this be for life. Will you please do something in my life so I that I can never say you don't exist?'

What I was asking him for was a miracle. I just sat there with my eyes tightly shut, waiting. It must have been after a few minutes' silence that Peter asked me, 'What are you waiting for?"

'The voice,' I replied.

'What voice?' he asked.

'The one you see and hear on those Moses films, where it sounds as if someone is talking into a bucket.'

He smiled and told me I didn't need to hear a voice; God had heard my prayer and had answered and would continue to answer. And even though I didn't hear the voice, I felt a peace in and around me that I had never felt before.

The news soon got around that the Northerner had

found God. People were congratulating and hugging me, which I found a little strange. The following day many asked me how I felt. I still had this peace in my life but also some doubts started to rise in my mind. Some people informed me that they had seen a huge difference in me the next day, especially at meal times. The difference was in my language. I was no longer swearing when asking someone to pass the salt or water; I had moved from 'effing and jeffing' to polite requests. Was this the miracle God was going to do? It certainly was. At school about 15 of us tried to stop swearing and failed. God was showing me that all he wanted to do was to remove the rubbish from my life and replace it with something better. I will never speak Queen's English or be on *University Challenge*, and I cannot say that I have never sworn since that day, but I can say that it is no longer habitual in my life.

I need to explain the type of person I was before I became a Christian: one big Approval Addict. Even though I had started a new life, I still carried this huge area of rejection with me, which affected my motives at times. I was one of those people who did not so much have a chip on his shoulder as a whole chip shop!

I just let rip and shouted, 'I've met God.'

The night I got home from this eventful week, I went straight back into the groove of things with my mates who had not been on the holiday. I was at a birthday party and we were drinking, dancing, and having a good time, when all of a sudden I felt I was going to explode with excitement. I knew I had to tell everyone what had happened. 'Be diplomatic,' I thought, when I just let rip and shouted,

'I've met God.' The response I got was amazing! Total silence. It was like someone had pressed the pause button. The dancing, drinking and laughing stopped and the staring began.

'You've met who?' asked someone.

'I've met God.'

Immediately there was uproar, from laughing to shouting obscenities.

Even though, from that day, I would face regular abuse or having the micky taken out of me, I was determined to still be there with my mates showing that God was real and that he had changed my life and could do the same for them. I continued to go to the pubs and clubs, played football and rugby, and continued to be their friend.

I wanted them to discover God too, but I felt quite isolated at times, especially at parties when they were getting drunk, sleeping around and fighting. Sometimes I felt I was missing out, even though I knew the opposite was true. My motivation for doing most things could be related to the need to be affirmed and told 'well done'. What I needed was a good dose of God and his love.

> Our self concept is determined not only by how we view ourselves but by how we think others perceive us. Basing our self worth on what we believe others think of us causes us to become addicted to their approval.
>
> We spend much of our time building relationships, striving to please people and win their respect. And yet, after all the sincere, conscientious effort, it takes only one unappreciative word from someone to ruin our sense of self worth. How quickly an insensitive word can destroy the self assurance we've worked so hard to achieve. (Robert McGee, *The Search for Significance*, Rapha Publications, 1990, pp. 63–64.)

In Romans 8:15–17 we read:

> For you did not receive a spirit that makes you a slave again to fear, but you received the Spirit of Sonship, and by him we cry 'Abba, Father.' The Spirit himself testifies with our spirit that we are God's children, that we are heirs, heirs with God and co-heirs with Christ, if indeed we share in his sufferings in order that we may also share in his glory.

In *The Message* it reads:

> The resurrection life you received from God is not a timid, grave-tending life. It's adventurously expectant, greeting God with a child-like 'What's next Papa?' God's Spirit touches our spirits and confirms who we really are. We know who he is and we know who we are: Father and children. And we know we are going to get what's coming to us – an unbelievable inheritance! . . . If we go through hard times with him, then we're certainly going to go through the good times with him!

It is true to say that insecurities hinder our relationship with God and our development as a person. My best mate Steve has often said, 'People are secure in their insecurities.' People can be so afraid to trust God and move out of their insecurities into the security of God. It sometimes seems easier to stay in our comfort zones, even if they cause us a lot of pain, than to move into something new – the amazing love of God. If you have difficulty doing this, you will fall into the trap of seeking man's approval and eventually become an expert in the Approval Addict cycle. This will then determine what your motives are.

I regularly fall into this trap and I'm so grateful for my wife Linda and my close friends who tell me when I do so.

As men of God we need to develop our intimacy with God and let him get closer to us.

I was once at a church meeting where the speaker was talking about how the church has created an environment of two groups of Christians: the professionals and the amateurs. This caused the majority of people to feel that they needed to be seen to be doing something at the front to be really accepted by God and the rest of the church. Again, this would reinforce the need to be approved for all those who struggle in this area.

The speaker went on to say that even though it has never been taught publicly from the front of most churches, the actions of the leaders speak for themselves. He produced a roll of tape the American police use when there has been an accident or crime committed, to put around the scene of the incident warning people that this is a restricted area. The words 'No unauthorised personnel beyond this point' were revealed as he and his wife unrolled the tape across the front of the church. He continued to explain that this is what the church and its leaders have done for centuries, not always by their words but often by their actions.

Many people feel like second-rate Christians, unauthorised . . . to go beyond a certain point.

This rang true with me as I recalled some of the conversations others had had with me recently about what they were or weren't allowed to do. The speaker continued that many people feel like second-rate Christians, unauthorised to do anything, due to a lack of encouragement or not being allowed to go beyond a certain point. He said that many felt that if they didn't get the opportunity to do something at the front of church they would never be fulfilled. He implied that this was a lie that would hold people back from achieving all that God had for them. He insisted that it is not about being seen up front but about being released and given permission to succeed with whatever God wants you to be involved with in the real place of need: the world.

As he and his wife held the tape at chest height, he encouraged those who related to what he had been speaking about to run through the tape and rip it up. He counted to three and nearly everyone ran to the front. Shouting, crying, stamping on the tape, people were doing business with God and allowing him to bring his freedom and healing to their lives. I was up there, ripping the tape, asking God to help me with the areas of my life where I fell into the trap of seeking man's approval. God did something powerful that day. I know the desire began in me to release the people of God into whatever God has for them and not hold them back. I have often failed, but it is still my passion.

I love the following quote by Martin Scott: 'Don't let the past dictate your future, but let the future dictate your present.' This can only happen when we put ourselves into a place where God is given permission to deal with the past. Most men are very good at keeping busy but not very good at sitting still. We need to discover the reality of Psalm 46:10: 'Be still and know that I am God.' As we do this, God can instil in us a holy confidence and security, which will help us to have purer motives in the things we do for him.

Is this what Jesus was trying to do when the 72 disciples returned excited about what had been happening? They returned with joy and said, 'Lord, even the demons submit to us in your name' (Luke 10:17).

> Jesus replied, 'I saw Satan fall like lightning from heaven. I have given you authority to trample on snakes and scorpions and to overcome all the power of the enemy; nothing will harm you. However, do not rejoice that the spirits submit to you, but rejoice that your names are written in heaven.'

I love being used by God whether it's sharing my story with people, working in schools, preaching, praying for people for healing, listening to people, prophesying, encouraging and releasing people, or giving people words of knowledge, especially outside the church setting such as pubs and restaurants. Whatever opportunity he gives me I love to do it. However, I have often acted like the disciples and returned home, blowing my own trumpet. Why? Because like most men, I am insecure.

Get a group of men together and listen to their conversation and you will soon be able to determine if they are secure in God or not. Quite often it ends up like the song 'Anything you can do, I can do better'. 'No, you can't.' 'Yes I can.' We try to outdo one another with the best story! Oh God, please help us. If we need any motivation to live and work for God, let it be because of what he has done for us. We have been given a new life, a brand new start – let's live as if we believe it. Let us be good news to others.

'You did not choose me, but I chose you and appointed you to go and bear fruit, fruit that will last' (John 15:16). This is what God says to all the men in the church. How fruitful are you?

One of the best motivators ever is the fact that you woke up this morning, still breathing! This means God still believes you can be useful for him. You have been given another chance to make a difference in this world and to someone else's life. Surely that must make you feel special?

> Motivation is an ever present influence in every sphere of your life. Your motives determine your enthusiasm and your satisfaction in every situation, whatever you are doing and wherever you are – at home, at work, with friends and even when you are alone. Motives are your constant companions. They have been with you since childhood. It is about time you became more acquainted! (George New and David Cormack, *Why Do I Do That?* Hodder & Stoughton, 1997.)

Questions

Please work through these questions, preferably with someone you know and trust.

1. What motivates you right now with your walk with God?
2. Have you recognised any areas of your life where you fall into being an 'Approval Addict'? Is there a regular pattern to this occurring?
3. How do you feel when you are with a group of men: secure or intimidated?
4. Do you feel your life is fruitful for God? If not, what changes do you need to make? What changes do you need to allow God to make?
5. Do you find it easy to be still in God's presence?
6. Are you 'good news' to be with?
7. Does the past dictate your future, or the future the present?

SELF-IMAGE

There is a lot of talk about self-image, and most of it to be honest is directed at women.

- Are men affected by self-image problems?
- What are our weak spots?
- What is body building all about?
- What about martial arts?

10

His Kingdom, Not Your Church?

LEE JACKSON

'He will always give you all you need from day to day if you will make the Kingdom of God your primary concern' (Luke 12:31 TLB).

If you're looking for a deep theological discussion about the kingdom, liberation theology, reconstructionism, dominion theology, dispensationalism, and other long words I could make up, then I'm afraid you're not going to find them in this chapter! In fact this is not the book to be reading – get a proper one! I have done some theological training, but I am by no means a theologian, as most if not all of my friends will tell you! In this chapter I'm going to just share some ideas on how a kingdom mindset slots into place for me, without even knowing it.

I am not mad!

I started on a course called 'Equipped to Lead' in September 1997. We met for a residential weekend in Derbyshire, with hundreds of other delegates starting a whole year of study in theology and practical leadership training, and for the first three or four sessions God spoke to me so much it was unbelievable. What he said was quite simply that I wasn't mad after all.

We were getting teaching on several issues around the kingdom of God and also Christo-centric theology, i.e. Jesus being the centre of everything we do. I hadn't known what I really thought about the kingdom of God, but I just realised that as an evangelist I saw myself as a kingdom-builder not a church-builder. This is quite strange because I am actually a very loyal member of a church. However, being kingdom-focused does not mean that you don't believe in local church, as one church leader I met thought. It just means that you believe in kingdom growth and not necessarily church growth (I hope this will stimulate some discussion!). As a friend of mine said, he'd read all the church growth books and he just didn't get it or want it! So as I sat being taught about the kingdom of God and different interpretations of it, it was fascinating to me that I had already come to these conclusions without ever having been taught the theology behind it. And 'Equipped to Lead', was for me just like putting some cement in the foundations that I had already built.

'The church is but the result of the coming of God's kingdom into the world by the mission of Jesus Christ.' (H. D. Wendland)

The kingdom is fascinating, as the present is bound up with the future. Linda Harding put it this way: 'We live between the already and the not-yet. Our inheritance is of the presence of the future. We already have the down payment, the guarantee, but there is still more to come.' One of the pastors featured in the *Transformations* video said, 'I realised that I wouldn't be held accountable for how I led my church, but for how I pastored my city.' The church leader who can think along those lines is very powerful indeed – one who looks to build their city, and the kingdom of God in their city and beyond.

Even though I want to stay in Leeds to see God move, I also feel the need to go and serve other places. For instance, I was involved in 'Message 2000' in Manchester, because I wanted to go and serve Manchester. If you know anything about the north of England, traditionally we sing rude songs about Manchester – we don't help them reach their city! The paradox is that as you dig deeper and seek to build the kingdom where you are, you actually get a wider view to break denominational barriers, break other boundaries, and serve people elsewhere. We are not Jesus to our church, we are Jesus to our city – and that influences everything we do.

I've done a lot of evangelistic activities and, if I am honest, they have mostly been about putting 'bums on seats' on Sunday morning. We must challenge ourselves to think, 'Can we do evangelism to build someone else's church, or even put people into a church experience which is far outside of our own?' That is where the rubber hits the road.

God still astounds me with the things he does. Many people just try to build their own little (or big) church, but God being God says, 'You go to build the kingdom, and build the city that you live in, and I will build my church in the process!' It's just the amazing grace that he has.

If the church is the body, as it says in 1 Corinthians 12, then the body must be used. We're told to *go* and bear fruit. And how does a body go and bear fruit? It needs to go and do things! (Sometimes I think I am too simplistic!) The body

---

'The church is the community of the kingdom but never the kingdom itself.'

---

of Jesus Christ needs to be active. We hear a lot about the church being the body of Christ, and different parts of it. I've even done assemblies in school about being the little finger of the body. But actually it's about putting the body into action. Ephesians 4:11 says this:

> 'And Christ gave gifts to people. He made some to be apostles, some to be prophets, some to go and tell the good news, and some to have the work of caring for and teaching God's people. Christ gave those gifts to prepare God's holy people for the work of serving to make the body of Christ stronger.' (New Century Version)

It's really interesting that Paul talks about the five-fold ministry as preparing God's people for the work of service, not just preparing God's people to be who they are. The church is not an end in itself but a springboard – a trampoline to serve God's kingdom. Any oppressive church leadership which says otherwise is holding back the kingdom of God.

Fragile

I've spent many hours in meetings with church leaders and it took me a while to realise how fragile some of their jobs are. Sometimes they are simply moving on; or sometimes they've been asked to leave where there's been a struggle that we didn't know was happening in the church; or it may be a moral issue. I'm not saying that this is true for everyone, but maybe some churches are not as radical as they could be because the leaders fear for their jobs, whether that's a paid job or whether that's a status involved in eldership or leadership. The most exciting, honest and open church leaders that I've met are the ones who have stuck their necks out for the sake of the kingdom.

In Leeds we have been involved in significant dialogues about working together, not in uniformity but in unity in some way, and it's so exciting to see how churches are willing to lay down some of their ideals for the sake of the kingdom. But you can also see people become very concerned for fear of their jobs and for fear of their whole theology and everything they've been taught over the last 10 or 20 years.

He said *go out*; not open the door and ask people to come in quietly, after they have wiped their feet.

Jesus didn't come, change us, and leave us to the work of having nice Sunday meetings. He left us with the Great Commission, that is to go out and tell people, and as St Francis of Assisi said, 'Use words if you have to.' Jesus didn't say have open services, or have services that are a bit more lively, and he certainly didn't say discuss for 17 hours whether you should start at 6.00 pm or 6.30 pm! He said *go out*; not open the door and ask people to come in quietly, after they have wiped their feet. That's a big difference, and a fundamental issue for a lot of churches in the West. A church that thinks that it's sorted always makes me nervous, and I often prefer the maverick style where people make mistakes but are actually trying to make a difference. Sure, it might not be a slick thing on a Sunday, or whatever day of the week, but it sorts out the men from the boys or the women from the girls.

I've been really blessed, in my schools work in Leeds, to have Leeds Faith In Schools financially supported by several of the churches. There are two particular churches I can think of who have given sacrificially to us, and that really blesses me because the kids we meet in schools are not necessarily going to end up in their youth groups. They just see that we're doing something in the city and they want to invest in that. It means they're giving money and they're not expecting a return on it. Do we sometimes give but hope that our giving will benefit *us* in some way? In Ephesians 4 Paul says that the body of Christ will be made stronger, but that comes after the works of service; so it's as we go out and serve that the church is built, which is the opposite way round to how we've often done it!

Working together

We have a great church in Leeds called Kidz Klub for unchurched 5–11s. The children are visited every week and taken by bus on a Saturday morning to Bridge Street Church in Leeds. Many churches have taken on a Kidz Klub and done it excellently (like Frontline Church in Liverpool), but Leeds started it with four or five churches, all paying for their own buses, and sending their own volunteers to be part of it. It's not owned by anybody, and it's simply building the kingdom of God in Leeds. Who knows what the future will bring from investment in these young people who, without that regular visit and bus ride, would never have heard the name of Jesus.

I get quite excited when I hear about 'mega-churches' and the impact they are having, but I'm much more stimulated by partnership and low-key networks that are seeking ways to serve the kingdom of God together. Howard Astin in Bradford is a great example of this. He is willing to network and invest into the Bradford area, but not necessarily for his own gain, and he's seen much fruit from that. His church isn't the biggest in the country, but I would certainly say it is one of the most effective.

The thing about kingdom values is that they affect you every single day. When making decisions about how to run Leeds Faith In Schools, I've managed to base them on kingdom values. A small charity like us often has to compete for funds from churches or from trusts, and I've decided to be open about where we get our money and how we apply for it, so as not to foster the kind of secret fundraising attitude a lot of small charities have.

The other thing that we're really keen on is sharing our ideas. Our website has got a list of all the videos and books and some of the ideas that we use on a day-to-day basis in school, with some comments from the workers, because we want to share it with people for the kingdom, and not just keep it to ourselves as our own private little enterprise. Nothing's original anyway, and if we're into building the kingdom then I'm happy to help someone in this country or other countries by passing on the things that God has taught us. 'There's no copyright in the kingdom' is a favourite schoolworker's line!

It's so easy to become entrenched in 'church, church, church', and not actually see the big picture. We're residents of a 'global village', and so we want to see the kingdom of God advance in the world. I want to see the kingdom of God advance in the West, in Europe, in the UK, in England, in Yorkshire, and in Leeds. In the big scheme of things, what I do isn't really that important. I don't want to be driven by a fundamental attitude of 'I want to build everything that's close to me', but rather have a kingdom value of 'Let's build this together'. That attitude should be natural to us, but often it isn't. But when you start to see things coming together, it really is very exciting, and I rejoice when I hear about other people's successes because that's what it's about. God has given to me, people have given to me, and I want to give back – it's as simple as that. If we are generous, God will be generous to us.

'The church is not here for me – but for the release of the kingdom.'

Questions

Check out Zechariah 8:20–21

1. What do you do that is not driven by kingdom values?
2. Can the local church exist if we *just* seek the kingdom?
3. If the research shows that people have a problem with church, will talking about the kingdom be helpful?
4. Do we have a distorted view of the relationship between the church and kingdom?
5. Did the disciples preach the kingdom or the church?

NOT A LOT!

On *The Heaven and Earth Show* on BBC 1, Paul Daniels (the magician) was asked about his life as a lay preacher when he was younger.

The one thing he struggled with, like many of us, is hypocrisy and the ridiculous religiousness in the church. In one of the chapels he used to go into, a certain lady would have a new hat every single week. She used to come to the church in the middle of the first hymn and everyone would stop and admire her lovely new hat. He knew this would happen so he made sure that he delayed the first song until *after* she had arrived! People used to wind her up about it and she found this very difficult especially as she was the wife of a local dignitary.

Amazingly it was little things like this that actually put him off church. Maybe he saw through the religion that so many of us think is part and parcel of what the church is about.

What is religion?

Do new churches suffer from it?

11

I'll Be There For You

Steve Halliwell

As my daughter and I sat in a café at a shopping complex after a long, hard, morning's shopping, we drank our coffee and watched people go by. There were ordinary people, older couples, young couples, lads on the prowl and, rather surprisingly, two men who were probably in their early thirties with their arm around each other laughing and joking as they headed towards the cinema. It seemed pretty obvious to my daughter and myself that these men weren't gay but they were strong friends.

I remarked to my daughter how unusual it was to see blokes just being affectionate to each other in public without there being any sexual connotations. It seems unusual sometimes to see men hugging each other, giving each other a kiss on the cheek or expressing how appreciative they are of each other's friendship. Maybe today's society doesn't encourage it because it is open to so much misinterpretation.

I consider myself to be a very fortunate man in a very happy relationship with my wife, and I have three gorgeous daughters. I am very privileged to say that I have seven extremely close male friends. I have known these friends for quite a number of years, and would feel comfortable embracing them and saying how much I love them. We express to each other the innermost secrets of our hearts and share our lives with each other on a very intimate level. A privileged man indeed to have such close friends. Of course I have other very good relationships, many of which are becoming the kind of relationships where we can share almost anything with each other.

As human beings we have very basic needs. We need to know that we're loved, that we are respected, that we can be ourselves and that we are appreciated. The need for friendship is one of the most basic we have. Sadly, it is one which many people are experiencing less and less. There are a number of reasons for this: first of all people are on the move a lot these days and therefore don't have time to build relationships as they did in the past. Second, there are risks involved in having friendships. You can be let down, betrayed and feel the pain and hurt of relationships that go sour.

There are many other reasons why it is difficult to build friendships. It could be that we are so insecure we feel nobody wants to be our friend, or maybe we feel that we cannot possibly be a good friend to someone else. The basic need for friendship never goes away.

Jesus encouraged friendships. Throughout the Bible we read of people who had very close relationships with each other. Jesus, of course, had his twelve disciples and his three intimate friends. The need for friendship and intimacy is highlighted to us clearly in the Scriptures and we feel it deeply in our hearts. So how can we form more meaningful friendships?

1. *Decide you want to be a friend.* So many people long for friendships and cry out to God or wail to other people that they have no friends. Of course the best way to make friends is to be a friend. Don't wait for people to ring you up – ring them first; buy something for them; do something for them. Make your mind up today to be a friend to someone. Go all out in doing everything you can for that person.

2. *Be yourself.* I have come to the conclusion that most people see right through any kind of pretence. I have found that people prefer the real me to the pretend me. People's antennas are quite sensitive and what they love to see in other people is something that they would like for themselves. It's important to be comfortable by being yourself.

3. *A little bit of honesty.* It is very important to say how you feel. It is equally important to be quite sensitive to the needs of other people. I sometimes have the problem of being far too honest, which brings about a shock reaction in people. All of a sudden they are faced with a person who is sharing far too much with them, far too quickly. Being appropriately honest is what people prefer.

4. *Vulnerability.* Linked with that little bit of honesty is a certain degree of vulnerability. A relationship that doesn't have all the answers, a person who hasn't got his life always together is the kind of person that people are quite attracted to and someone they want to spend time with. When a person can share their struggles honestly and be vulnerable, there is a tendency for others to respond sensitively and with great understanding.

5. *Time.* Friendships really do take considerable time. People don't trust themselves totally to someone quickly. That seems right. If we are interested in more than superficiality in our relationships with each other, it will take time to build up trust. It takes time to see whether or not the person we are hoping to have a deep friendship with can take the things that we might have to say to them, and the only way to find that out is the test of time.

6. *Patience.* In the friendships that I have had for a number of years, many of them have been tested almost to beyond endurance. I have constantly been faced with the issue of whether I should just give up on them. Patience has kept me going. First, I have thought that maybe I am just as bad as they are. Second, I have thought that I wouldn't want anyone to give up on me, so I am not going to give up on them.

7. *You don't have to say a lot.* Some of the best times I have had with my closest friends have been when things didn't need to be said. Often I would be in the situation where I just wanted someone to listen. The last thing I wanted was advice or information – I just needed someone to be there. Real friends don't judge or criticise, or necessarily provide any kind of counsel. Often people simply need to be allowed to say 'Can I tell you how I really feel?' without the fear of being rejected.

The whole issue of friendship is just about that. It's about knowing that you are not going to be rejected for what you have or have not done; for what you have or have not said. Friendships and relationships are about forgiveness. They are about being the kind of person that you would want to be around. Jesus tells us to treat other people in the way we would like to be treated. My advice in any kind of relationship is this – put yourself in someone else's shoes if you can and recognise that it is always better to give than to receive. It is the only way forward to having deep, meaningful relationships.

Questions

1. Have you got at least one close male friend you can be yourself with?
2. What do you look for in a friend?
3. Are you this kind of friend to others?
4. What areas do you struggle with in friendships?
5. Can you be yourself with your friends? If not, why not?
6. Can you tell your friends anything and know they will still love you?
7. Have you ever felt rejected by your friends? How did you rectify this?
8. How easily do you find it to show your love physically towards your male friends?
9. On a scale of 1–10, how would you rate yourself as a friend?

INTIMACY

I've been thinking about what gay men have to teach us about being men (not that I'm . . . no, no, not me . . . I watch football, me!), because it seems to me that if you've ever had the privilege of being welcomed into the gay community, you'll find among all the queer-as-folk soap operas that it's quite like church. Only better. A bit like Christians, gay men have to stick together to protect themselves and look after each other, but they seem to do it so much better than many of us. I wonder (and I realise this might be a contentious point) if they are more sure of who they are than we are. I'm also acutely aware that they have something that some of us don't: intimacy between men. I've even heard it argued that lots of gay men aren't really homo-*sexual* at all, they just want some intimacy with a man – something which our culture pretty much forbids.

I remember going to Freshers' Fair at university. There was a guy running a stall and – even now I'm embarrassed to admit it in print – I found him really attractive. I didn't want to kiss him, let alone all the other stuff. I just wanted to be close to him. Needless to say, I ran a mile. 'Oh Lord, am I gay?' I wailed inwardly. And to be fair, the gay lobby haven't helped. Turning David and Jonathan's friendship ('they loved each other with a love greater than the love of women') and the medieval contracts of friendship based on that biblical model into 'evidence' that God and the church have always blessed gay sex is just ludicrous. We need to recover a biblical understanding of male intimacy that totally sidesteps sexuality altogether. Because despite all this 'new man' stuff, we do have a problem with letting down our defences.

(Simon Hall)

12
Keep On Keeping On
LEE JACKSON

Youth workers often stay in their job for only two to three years, so the statistics say. When things get difficult, or life is pressured, it's often easier to move on – and this is a struggle that I've dealt with over the last few years.

Haven't you left yet?

In my job with Leeds Faith in Schools, my trustees are really surprised that I've been in the job for eight years now. Leeds is a place where I want to be, and where we are going to stay unless we get a signed postcard from God telling us otherwise! This flies in the face of traditional youth work, where you go and do your stuff for a couple of years and then you can move on. And actually the sadness of this, as Paul Borthwick pointed out, is that you can have maybe three years' worth of good ideas, then when you run out, you can always go somewhere else and use those ideas again. So 14 years down the road, you're still trying out the same ideas you had 14 years ago. This is an easy thing to slip into as a youth worker, especially as you've got to be inspired and an ideas-driven kind of person. But what is getting me excited more than anything else at the moment is people who just say: 'God's called me here, and I'm staying!' Just standing still is sometimes warfare – never mind moving forward.

It may be a lot more exciting to travel the world and go to different places. However, that has never had the same attraction for me as staying where I am and seeing God transform the place where I live. And thankfully in Leeds there are a lot of people who feel the same way, and we're here to see this through. I have the privilege of being with people who have been here for 30 years or more, and are still waiting for God to move in the city of Leeds. Martin Scott says, 'This is a bad time to give up.' You may think this is kind of obvious, but actually it is very good advice. This is a bad time to give up, because you haven't seen it through. You haven't seen what God has to do. It's always a bad time to give up! In the George Otis Jnr. book *Transformations* he states that in all cases of God transforming a community there are two common factors: 1. persevering leadership and 2. fervent informed intercession. We must learn to fuel the fire within us (or maybe just light it!).

> Our goal is unashamedly territorial. It is to see the will of God expressed in a particular patch of earth. We will not be vague in our praying, but focused, looking for the coming of the kingdom where we are. We will seek God for revelation about what is hindering the coming of that kingdom, with the full awareness that he gives revelation in proportion to what we can affect. (Martin Scott, *Sowing Seeds for Revival*, Renew 2002)

'The good influence of godly citizens causes a city to prosper, but the moral decay of the wicked drives it downhill' (Proverbs 11:11 TLB). I'm not saying we shouldn't have travelling missions groups and itinerant ministries. But these people should be unusual, and we should see the majority of people staying where they are, praying and trying to make a difference. I have a friend who is extremely gifted – certainly more gifted than I am in many areas (except DJ-ing!). But the shame is that over the last few years I have seen him move from place to place, and I just wonder what he has achieved and what moves him on. People might not be excited about me being here in Leeds for twelve years and working with the same young people and schools for eight years, but I just think that God's heart is to dig deep and get your hands dirty. The deeper you dig, the harder it gets but the closer you are. Maybe the secret is to stay and get more passionate, and not to move on when the passion wears out.

Test of faith

I was involved in a big church event in Leeds recently where I was the compere. It was there I had one of the strangest experiences of my life, which really has affected me. I spent the previous two weeks talking at a youth celebration in Leeds about the cost of discipleship and the fact that people give their lives for Jesus all the time in other countries, and, as Ed Silvoso says, maybe it's time to reclaim that gift of martyrdom. So there I was right in the centre of Leeds, right in the hub of the city, leading this celebration, and I suddenly had a fear that I might lose my life there and then. I suddenly thought that all it takes is one nutter, one idiot to make a mistake, to do something silly, stupid or intentional, and that could be it for me in this public arena. And for a whole week afterwards, this totally wiped me out. It was the first thing I thought about in the morning, and the last thing I thought about at night, and it's something I'm still really wrestling with God about.

'Don't worry about a thing, 'cos every little thing gonna be alright! Don't give up the fight!' (Bob Marley)

A few years ago, Justin and I were rehearsing a song at the 'Event for Revival' in Norfolk. It was an afternoon rehearsal and sound check. All five of us were rapping together, and all of a sudden out of nowhere this man appeared, fists flying. He attacked me and Mark Pennels, grabbed Justin's microphone, and used it to hit him on the jaw. He hit him so hard that Justin had the imprint of the microphone on his cheek for a couple of days afterwards! Obviously the noise had been too much for him. I think he had been camping nearby and he just flipped, and that was it! We had to sit on him in the end to calm him down and try to find the people he was with. There were stewards and security people there, but it still happened.

Apathy has almost killed the Western church.

Whenever you do anything publicly, you always leave yourself open to people with strange ideas, or even psychiatric problems that may spark them off to do something crazy. It's funny, but in those times your faith is put to the test –

those are the times when you realise what you do and don't believe. A lot of Western Christians have never had the opportunity to have their faith tested, so they probably don't know what to believe, or worst of all they are just apathetic or not particularly bothered. Apathy has almost killed the Western church.

Staying where you are and digging in where God's called you is to experience something of the heart of God. God is faithful, and we should be too. It's as simple as that. We should not be people who move on from one thing to another. I learnt very quickly during my time with Youth With A Mission that you make where you are your home. Even in the five months that I was there, we carried photographs and personal belongings around with us, and wherever we were that night I used to put up my photographs to make it my home and not have the view that *I'm just drifting through*. Wherever I am, whether it's for years or for days, I try to make my home there and make the most of it.

'And work for the peace and prosperity of Babylon. Pray for her, for if Babylon has peace so will you' (Jeremiah 29:7 TLB). God likes to work things out through people and relationships. This is where our reality kicks in because our faith in God is tested in difficult and in day-to-day situations. God roots us in people and in places. His character is not fly-by-night. If you want an example of this, look at the people of Israel in Exodus. Why was God so faithful to Israel when they wandered around the desert? Why was he so faithful to them when they made images of idols while Moses met with God (Exodus 32)? It's because it's in God's nature. He's here for the long-term, for the long haul. He's beyond time anyway, so it makes no difference to him! He wants us to dig in.

'We have to pray from within because we too belong to the city. Where we live is our city, our place.' (Martin Scott)

I've worked in the same schools for eight years now, which is longer than half the staff because of the high turnover rate. At least I can't be accused of being a mad proselytising evangelist, because I'm there week after week! God is blessing me and showing me his faithfulness, and I find people are more open to God when they see I am here for them for the long-term. Recently a teacher in a school gave me a Technics turntable worth about £250 for my DJ work. He said, 'I want to give it to you in appreciation for the work you've done in school.' He didn't fall on his knees and say, 'How can I be saved?' But he recognised what I am doing in school is making a difference in people's lives. Do not underestimate the gift of perseverance.

When Steve Chalke was asked, 'What's your greatest gift?' he simply said, 'I think my greatest gift is that I'm a plodder. I just get on with it day by day – keep pushing it, keep doing it. . .' That's exactly the sort of person I want to be. I make mistakes, but I've got to keep plodding on – it's as simple as that. Sometimes being a Christian is an act of will, especially when heaven appears silent. You have to put your faith into action, and not just expect fluffy nice feelings to come your way. The best way not to give up is just not to give up!

When Winston Churchill was invited back to his old school, it was a great moment for them all as the head teacher introduced one of the greatest public speakers and one of the most influential people of recent times, Churchill was given a huge build up! He worked his way to the front of the stage in typical shuffling style, looked at the young men sitting before him and simply said: 'Never give up. Never, never, never, never, never give up.' And then he sat down! Imagine the faces of the robed teachers expecting a 30-minute inspirational speech! And so a man with all his faults managed to capture something of the heart of God, and the perseverance we need in order to live out our lives.

We have instant gratification in our society: instant coffee, instant meals, instant everything. In fact we're not happy unless we've got at least 27 channels of repeats on TV to flick through at any one time. But actually some things are worth waiting for, and I'm waiting here in Leeds for the time when God comes like he's promised.

In a study of the history of religion in Leeds, the introduction says, 'The most remarkable thing about the history of religion in Leeds is that nothing remarkable has ever happened!' (This is not strictly true if you consider that Smith Wigglesworth had his first experience of miraculous healing here!) If you know you're going to be somewhere for the rest of your life, maybe you'll make each day count.

This note was found in the office of a young pastor in Zimbabwe following his martyrdom for his faith in Jesus Christ. Read and meditate on this if you dare.

> I'm part of the fellowship of the unashamed. I have the Holy Spirit power. The die has been cast. I have stepped over the line. The decision has been made – I'm a disciple of his. I won't

look back, let up, slow down, back away, or be still. My past is redeemed, my present makes sense, my future is secure. I'm finished and done with low living, sight walking, smooth knees, colourless dreams, tamed visions, worldly talking, cheap giving and dwarfed goals.

I no longer need pre-eminence, prosperity, position, promotions, plaudits or popularity. I don't have to be right, first, tops, recognised, praised, regarded or rewarded. I now live by faith, lean in his presence, walk by patience, am uplifted by prayer, and I labour with power.

My life is set, my gait is fast, my goal is heaven, my road is narrow, my way rough, my companions are few, my guide reliable, my mission clear. I cannot be bought, compromised, detoured, lured away, turned back, deluded or delayed. I will not flinch in the face of sacrifice, hesitate in the presence of the enemy, pander at the pool of popularity, or meander in the maze of mediocrity.

I won't give up, shut up, let up, until I have stayed up, stored up, prayed up, paid up, preached up for the cause of Christ. I am a disciple of Jesus. I must go till he comes, give till I drop, preach till all know, and work till he stops me. And, when he comes for his own, he will have no problem recognising me. My banner will be clear!

Questions

1. Have you ever feared for your life?
2. Why do our prayers for a place mean more if we are living there? Get a copy of The Vision from www.24-7prayer.com and pray it if you believe.
3. Are you a 'two-year' boy?
4. What is drifting through? Are you doing it?

COMMANDMENTS FOR LIVING

1. Don't let life happen to you – live with purpose.
2. Everyone has self-doubt – learn to be comfortable with yourself.
3. Don't whinge about what you can't do – enjoy what you can do.
4. *Every* man struggles with sexual sin – don't hide it, be honest with other men.
5. Don't waste time trying to 'prove' something – just be yourself and enjoy life.
6. There is no 6.
7. If you can, find a good woman and marry her – she will make you complete.
8. Be fanatical about Jesus – devote your life to being like him.
9. Don't be afraid to fail – the only person who never failed never did anything.
10. Don't waste your time criticising others or being angry or bitter – life's too short.
11. Read the Bible as often as you can – it will keep you alive longer.
12. Never say never – things change for good and bad!
13. Never lose your perspective or sense of humour – if you haven't got one, get one!
14. Life's a journey. Try and enjoy the ride.
15. Get some good friends and keep them – you'll need them sooner or later.
16. Try to do at least one crazy or impetuous thing a year – keep 'em guessing!

(Jonathan)

13

Never Been Trained!

LEE JACKSON

It's Father's Day when I'm writing this chapter, and I've sneaked up to my office to get some thoughts down while Lauren is asleep. That's the great thing about having twins – they're not usually both asleep at the same time, so you're always on the go. Some people have called it 'double trouble', or 'trial by fire'! Rhea and Lauren are our first and last children! We have no history of twins in our family, so it came as quite a shock, and we believe that God spoke through their birth. Rhea and Lauren are identical twin girls, three years old at the moment, and they're amazing. But sometimes they are just plain hard work; more difficult for me than Clare, as men seem to handle kids very differently to the way women do!

'Most men are just not designed to look after children for more than 20 minutes at a time. By about 25 minutes, the man's usually lost interest, he's watching television, and the children are in the kitchen microwaving car batteries!' (Jack Dee)

Being a dad is an experience I never could have prepared for. Here are a few thoughts, not deep theological theories, about being a dad.

People never say on their deathbed, 'I wish I'd spent more time at the office.' (Rob Parsons)

Andy Hickford said, 'I'm the best father in the world . . . when I'm away from home.' I and many of my friends can completely sympathise with that. I often find it very hard being at home with Rhea and Lauren, because it's especially difficult when you've got things to do. But the amazing thing is that I miss them loads as soon as I get to work, or as soon as I go away. That in itself has made me think about my attitude when I'm at home. It's so easy to forget the wonderful gift that children are to us.

I went with Clare to the hospital when she went for her first ultrasound scan. We waited with all the other parents surrounded by 'breast is best' posters! It was the first thing on a Monday morning, and we were the first scan of the week. The radiologist was warming up the machine, she put the ultrasound sensor on Clare's stomach with that nasty greasy stuff, and immediately she said, 'I've got something to tell you – you're having twins!' Clare and I just looked at each other, completely aghast, and Clare gently started to cry (I think tears of joy!). It was amazing as the nurse gradually described how they were lying and how they were intertwined with each other, and whose leg was whose and which arm was which! Those ultrasound pictures still look like ink blots to me, but being there and seeing them in motion, I could actually work out limbs, heads and even the heart.

So things were fairly straightforward as far as the pregnancy was concerned, apart from Clare being very big. It got to the point, towards the end, where she could have carried a wheelbarrow in front of her just to take the load off for a while! With seven weeks to go, we had started to clear the spare room out for the babies, including my DJ equipment (boo!), but hadn't really bought anything for them yet. We went to bed as normal, with Clare stacking herself up with pillows and trying to get herself comfortable. Then between 5 and 6 in the morning, I heard these very quiet words, 'Lee, I think my waters have broken.' I suddenly burst into action getting up, getting ready, getting towels, doing all the things I thought I had to do, and if any of you have ever met me before, you'll realise that I'm not usually awake before midday! So this was quite an achievement, and all of a sudden there we were – babies on the way, nothing bought, and a risk of the babies being dangerously small as they were very premature. It was such a strange feeling, suddenly realising that I was going to be a dad, and I think I must have gone into autopilot, just going through the motions.

Clare went into labour (while being pumped with steroids) but there was no room at the inn! The special care baby units in Leeds were full, so we waited for a couple of hours while they rang round different hospitals, and in the end we had to go to Manchester. Clare went in an ambulance with the blue lights flashing, and I was told to follow behind – *slowly* – without jumping any red lights. I was gutted!

It was a normal delivery and they just needed a little bit of help at the end to come out. Rhea was the first. She was wrapped up tightly because she was so small and all we could see were these two little eyes looking at us. It was amazing to think, 'I've created a human being!' She was then whisked away, to be cared for and within seven minutes Lauren came out, which is quite typical – she likes to sleep a lot more than Rhea does! We had a quick look at her before she too was whisked away. We didn't see them for a few hours after that until they were stabilised and assessed.

Nothing could have prepared me for the next six weeks of going into the special care unit, machines bleeping all around us, and occasionally alarms going off, followed by mad rushes of doctors with babies in their arms. It was a very harsh introduction to being a dad – especially as I lived off hospital food! We prayed a lot for them in the first few weeks. They were always rigged up to alarms which would often go off for various reasons, and that kept us on edge all the time. While Clare was in hospital with Rhea and Lauren, I had to run around buying things like cots, buggies, blankets and whatever else we needed, as we just hadn't had the opportunity to buy anything at all. My life had changed for ever. Becoming a parent is the one thing that really changes your life, and something that you're not usually trained for.

Now Rhea and Lauren are doing well. They are well-developed normal kids and they are a joy to be with (most of the time!). I often have to remind myself of the early days when we didn't know whether Rhea and Lauren would live or die, or whether they would have severe disabilities – always a risk for premature babies. And now when they're climbing all over the furniture and digging into my record bag, and calling 999 on my mobile, it's difficult to think back and remember what a gift they are!

Perhaps, that's the problem. We don't think back, we

don't remember how amazing it was in those first few days – that new feeling of being a dad, friends bringing you cigars and taking you out to wet the baby's head . . . that can all get lost in the day-to-day, early mornings, late nights and the pooey nappies.

'Baby poo is one part Velcro and one part nuclear waste.' (Robin Williams)

Fatherhood isn't talked about much in most Christian circles. Do we pretend we are good fathers when really we feel it's a hard slog sometimes? Hearing some honesty from people about how difficult they find it has been helpful for me.

Many researchers say that women are able to be 'multi-tasking'. They can do more than one thing at once, and do them all pretty well! But most men have less of that ability, so we must concentrate on one thing at once. When we're looking after children, that's what we must do. And that's difficult when we've got other things on our mind, or we're distracted. I'm amazed at the multi-tasking of my mam, who has looked after the girls when I'm at work, and has also managed to shampoo the carpet, clean the oven, and decorate one of the rooms in the house! How she does it, I'll never know. Keeping children entertained is one of the hardest things I've ever had to do, especially combined with the false Christian guilt that you're not meant to be entertaining them, you're meant to be educating them in a godly way. There can be so much pressure on Christian parents that it's quite hard sometimes just to enjoy yourself with your children. Seeing light at the end of the tunnel is the way we've found it with twins. We jokingly say sometimes that one baby must be a doddle! It certainly is like being dropped in at the deep end, and if it wasn't for the help of our good friends, and especially our family, we may have sunk instead of swum over the last three years!

Becoming a parent tests what you really do believe. There is a danger that people can end up living their lives through their children, or as Bertrand Russell said, 'The fundamental defect of fathers is that they want their children to be a credit to them.' The insecurities you kept hidden as an adult often come out in you as a parent. So how can we as men become fathers, and good fathers at that?

'To become a father is not hard . . . but to be a father is very hard.' (Wilhelm Bush)

I look back to the way my dad dealt with me, and I'm amazed sometimes at the way he gave me so much freedom but still managed to correct me when I needed it. And I hope that I can find that balance of allowing freedom so I don't become over-protective, and also steer and guide my children gently to make the right decisions and to live the radical life. I remember Jeff Lucas saying his faith was tested when his grown-up daughter went off to Africa to do a mission trip, even though she was doing just exactly what he'd been preaching for the last 20 years. I appreciate honesty like that, and believe fathers need to get together more often to share some of the struggles and joys of this fatherhood business.

An attitude of gratitude

Trying to maintain the right attitude is often half the battle. Having twins provokes all sorts of reactions in people, but one of the strangest in my life was when I was walking with

Rhea and Lauren in the buggy together and someone stopped us. Usually people coo over the girls and ask the same questions again and again, but this person just stopped and shook his head. 'Phew,' he said. 'That must be hard work . . .', and he walked off!

I used to know a guy who had just had kids and you would have thought he had got a disease! I never heard a positive word from him, and as his kids were slightly older than mine he used to be the prophet of doom. 'Wait until they get their injections'; 'Wait until they get their first teeth!'

Yes, it is hard work, but Clare and I need to keep the attitude that they are an amazing gift and it is a privilege to bring up two young women of God. In fact it's the most important job that we can ever do – to invest our lives into our children. Before you become a dad, talk to one!

'The world doesn't need father figures; it needs dads.'

Questions

1. Do you enjoy your kids?
2. In the book *Man and Boy*, Tony Parsons suggests that there are new starts when we get it wrong, but the dream is still to get it right first time. Discuss.
3. How does your relationship with your dad affect your relationship with your kids?

MEN OF A CERTAIN AGE

I see so much gifting in older men in the church. Those of us over 50 years collectively have a wealth of talent, experience, finance and stability. What a resource and one that's so desperately needed by the body: to disciple those young in the faith, to parent the fatherless, to release and support frontline ministries. And yet what is the reality; what do we find when the fruits of many in this generation are weighed? A bunch of old farts who sit in congregations and stand for very little? A resource that's locked up by self-interest and lethargy? Come on men 'of a certain age'! We must repent of our passivity before the Lord. We need to be released by the Holy Spirit from the trappings of the world that bind us in. There are many thousands of us in Britain. We could easily provide a platform that would bring the kingdom of God to this land. But will we, or will the devil say of those who stand against him, 'I know of these women and children, but who are you?'

(Chris)

14

Never On a Sunday

Baz Gascoyne

Ever since my fifth birthday, sport has been a passion of mine. Memories of my first football and football boots are still vivid. I would spend hours in the cobbled back alley kicking a football against the wall and dreaming of the day when I would become a professional footballer. At the age of eleven, I had the privilege of playing a cup final at Darlington Football Club ground, again reinforcing what I wanted to do when I left school.

Senior school introduced me to so many sports: athletics, basketball, cricket, football, rugby, soft ball, swimming, and volleyball became part of my weekly sporting diet. In the classroom I felt insecure and incapable of achieving, but outside I felt free – able to do something well and excel in it.

At the age of 15, I had a trial for a professional football club. Was my dream about to become a reality? The answer was a big NO! On the third day at the club, while doing some physical training, the player coach sexually interfered with me. Confused and angry I left the club without saying anything to anyone. My dream had been snatched away without my being given a proper chance to give it my best shot. I struggled with the comments from friends and family offering me their advice for the future, when they were oblivious to what had happened. I did not dare tell my mother, as she is built like Pat of *EastEnders* and would probably have gone with a pair of pliers to castrate the guy! My mates would just find something amusing to say about it.

I continued to play sports, especially football and rugby. My behaviour on the field became more aggressive and erratic, as I struggled with what had happened.

Sunday sport

Something else I struggled with was the issue of priorities. In the African and Caribbean Evangelical Alliance magazine, November 1999 – January 2000, there was an article entitled 'Sunday – A Day to Pray or Play'. The article was about a young boy named Samson and his parents, and the tension caused by Samson's desire to play football on a Sunday rather than go to church. On occasions his parents would physically escort him to church. Samson's mother was quoted as saying, 'I am so upset Samson has chosen football over the Lord. We are a God-fearing family who do not expect this to be the case.'

I need to say at this point that I am not a parent yet so I do not know how Christian parents feel when this problem arises. However, I do believe that children, teenagers and adults are not usually choosing between sport and God but between sport and the church. And in most cases there is no contest. Sport wins hands down! Why? Maybe because church is not relevant for these people and they get their love, support and encouragement from their colleagues, which to them is their church.

One of the things I struggled with more than anything else when I became a Christian was the way a few people made it clear that they were not happy with me playing sport if it interfered with church attendance. This became a huge problem for me, as football was such a large part of my life. I loved playing the game, but also needed the friendships I had acquired over the years through football. What was God's view on this? Did he want me to stop, or continue with his help to show my friends the difference he had made to my life? Surely this was better than packing the game in and isolating myself from them by being consumed into the Christian ghetto.

He bought me a sew-on cotton badge for the front of my football shirt, with the words 'Jesus is my Lord'.

One of my friends, who attended the same church, decided to help me with witnessing to my football colleagues. He bought me a sew-on cotton badge for the front of my football shirt, with the words 'Jesus is my Lord'. He said it would give me plenty of opportunities to talk about my faith in God. So, as a naïve teenager eager to do the right thing, I asked my grandmother to sew it on for me. My friend was right. It gave me plenty of opportunities – to be embarrassed and receive a barrage of obscenities and sarcasm! Every week I would hear the same phrases repeated: 'It's Bible basher Baz'; 'There's Moses'; 'Gascoyne has got religion'; and some not repeatable. The biggest challenge for me became how quickly I could cover the badge with mud after leaving the changing room. This only increased my sense of guilt and condemnation, feeling I was letting God down by being a poor witness.

I remember once I needed to go to the loo before we kicked off at a match I was playing in. As there were no toilets around, I just went behind the goal to relieve myself. As I was enjoying myself, my manager shouted over to me, 'Call yourself a Christian doing that!' I looked over at him in amazement, which was a mistake as I peed on my leg and socks.

After the match I asked my manager what he meant by his comment. He thought now that I was a Christian I would not want to do the same as the rest of the players. We had a laugh together when I replied, 'Christians still need to go to the toilet just like anyone else.' After that incident John and I got on really well.

Later that year the manager's youngest son died, and we were able to have some deep talks together. He asked me to pray for his wife, children and himself. I believe that came about from just being myself and trying to show something of God's love in the way I trained, played and befriended the other guys despite all the banter because of my faith.

I wish I could say that I have always been a good example on the football pitch and never let myself or God down. I used to play for three different teams during the weekend, on Saturday afternoon, Sunday morning and Sunday afternoon. The team I played for on Saturday had the highest standard of football but it was also the area where I got into the most trouble. There was one person I played against who was five years older than me. Every time we played he would start a fight with me. I would ask God to help me show something of God's love to him, by not reacting or retaliating when he fouled me deliberately or punched me when the referee was not looking. I would usually manage this, but then one match I failed big time. I had just received the ball with my back to the goal when this guy came flying in to tackle me and took both my legs away from under me with no intention of trying to get the ball. I could feel the anger rising as I slowly tried to get up. I thought to myself, 'OK God, I apologise now for what I am going to do!' As I got up I stretched out one of my legs. I knew this guy was still behind me and I caught him right in the throat with my boot. Still not looking back I slowly jogged away running off my injury, pretending I didn't know what had happened. When I eventually looked round this guy was lying on the grass receiving some assistance from their coach.

I remember talking to my youth leader about how I didn't want to lose my temper while playing football or mess up any opportunities of witnessing. Bill just told me to apologise when I did wrong but said, 'Don't allow yourself to be walked all over just because people think you are going to be a soft touch because of your new found faith.'

I only played for the Sunday morning team when the first choice keeper was away or injured. I played in goal as my second position, only because no one else was daft enough to. At the end of one season I was asked to play the final game of the season. Whoever won this won the league. Our opponents had a few ex-professionals in their team and were favourites to win. It's amazing how pumped up you can get when someone tells you we don't expect to win.

One of the opponents I was not pleased to see was a guy who deliberately broke my ankle three years previously. Unfortunately ten minutes into the game I made a mistake from which they scored. There must have been about 75 people watching this match, all shouting their opinions.

Next thing I knew my fist had made contact with his face.

Fortunately with 30 minutes to go we scored to equalise. From then on the tempo increased. I came out to intercept a pass that had been put through to one of their forwards. As I picked the ball up the forward followed through with his boot and caught me on the leg. As I stood there looking at him, he swore at me and punched me in the face. Immediately there was a shout from the touch line from a few of my friends, 'Chin him Baz' (meaning punch him back). It was just like my brain went into auto pilot and next thing I knew my fist had made contact with his face and he was lying on the grass. Immediately I thought of the 'Jesus is Lord' badge on my shirt, so I pulled the ball up to my chest as the referee approached. I was waiting to be sent off when he just told us both to grow up and get on with the game. The match ended in a draw.

At the end of the match I went up to the forward and apologised for what I had done. I explained I had become a Christian and should not have reacted like that. His response was, 'It's OK mate. I deserved it.' Because of the draw, we had to play a replay the following Tuesday. As the keeper was on holiday I played in that match as well. The match was more physical than the previous one, and I asked God to help me play to the best of my ability and not lose my temper. Both prayers were answered. We finished 4-2 and won the league. The victory was made even sweeter when we discovered that our opponents were on £50 per man and we were on a pint of whatever we wanted from the local club.

I tell you those two stories just to emphasise the pressure and the problems that can arise for Christian men, young or old, while taking part in a competitive sport. I do believe that Christianity and competitive sports are compatible. However, we need to be honest about our struggles and make sure we allow God into this area of our lives.

Sport is a fantastic way of getting alongside people, whether it's during training, playing a match, a round of golf or just watching. Whatever your interest, playing, coaching or watching, remember to enjoy it to the full and allow God to use you, your gift and the forum he has given to you. A book I would highly recommend is *What the Book Says About Sport* by Stuart Weir from Christians in Sport.

Questions

1. Is winning the most important thing to you?
2. Do you have a problem controlling your anger while playing? What are you doing about it?
3. If you do have a problem in this way, would it be wise to give up playing your sport for a while?
4. Has your church ever thought about doing a sport's day as an outreach? How could you help organise this?
5. Is it wrong for Christians to defend themselves while playing a sport, or should they turn the other cheek?
6. How far would you go to win? Would you cheat or break the rules? Would you injure someone else for your cause?

7. Should Christian men be involved in playing sports on a Sunday?
8. Is it true that most Christian football leagues are worse for disciplinary actions than those leagues that are not?
9. Can you lose a game and still enjoy your sport?

DAY BY DAY

If prayer is a lifestyle
If worship is a lifestyle
If loving people is a lifestyle
If discipleship is a lifestyle
If mission is a lifestyle . . .
Why do I only do CHURCH on a Sunday?

(Tim)

15
Sorry to Bother You . . .

Lee Jackson

What's the slowest thing on four legs?. Two Christians trying to get through a door! What's this?: 'Oo, sorry' . . . 'Oo, sorry' . . . 'Oo, my mistake' . . . 'Oo sorry' . . . 'Oo' . . . 'Please forgive me.' The bumper cars at a Christian conference! (A Tim Vine joke.)

'What the world needs is people who are alive.' (Gil Bailie)

It seems that most British people think we should be totally polite the whole time, and so a British person who is also a Christian is probably the politest and the 'nicest' person you've ever met – certainly in public, anyway! This cultural absurdity was brought to light in the TV programme *The Human Zoo*, where a group of people were asked to stay in a room until someone came to collect them. A fake fire was set off in the next room, and smoke poured in. The smoke alarm went off, but no one moved! They were just too polite and too embarrassed to do anything about it, and the fire officers in attendance said that if the fire had been real they would have been dead within four minutes!

Bulldog spirit

When I met Ivan and Isobel Allum from Toronto, they gave me a ten-minute prophecy that said I was to be a 'brawler' in the kingdom of God. The prophecy didn't say I was to be 'a nice lovely man of God', but a fighter – a man of violence in the kingdom of God. Another prophecy I received was that someone saw me as a British bulldog! He didn't know I was English at the time. I thought to myself, 'That's not very polite – surely he means I'm a nice man of God . . . !' But no – he said, 'You are a British bulldog, and you are standing in front of young people and you're protecting them from the enemy.' So immediately after that I did some research on bulldogs and also found a picture of a bulldog for my office desk. The original dogs were not like the ones we see now with breathing and skin problems because of over-breeding, but they were actually used as fighting dogs and for bull baiting. Their jaws were strong enough to grab a bull by its nose and hold it still while the farmer did whatever he had to do. And once they had hold, they wouldn't let go even to the point of death. They were full of tenacity and didn't give up.

Over the last few years, I've had some funny stares and fingers being pointed at me when I've been in meetings and conferences, not only because of the occasional strange haircut, but because I often take a drum to worship God and to pray over people. I would pound this Dolak (an Indian drum) as hard as I could, and put the drumstick onto people's stomachs when I prayed for them. It wasn't a polite or nice thing to do, but something I felt was needed. Also, as mentioned previously, I occasionally carry round a replica (metal not plastic!) of the *Braveheart* sword, which Mel Gibson used in the film.

This doesn't fit with English reserve or with a traditional view of Christian men, but it's been an enormous help to me to rely on these weapons of war in the real fight that I'm here for in Leeds.

I have some great friends who have really got a 'warrior spirit'. Baz is an example of that, as well as my friends Caleb and Tim, who literally fight their way to God. They push through and are not afraid to make mistakes – and believe me, we have all made quite a few of those!

The Bible is a radical book, but we've managed to make it 'nice' and sterile over the years. A classic example of this is the Good Samaritan in Luke 10. There have been many different versions of this, and I remember in the eighties the drama of 'the good punk rocker', where the Samaritan would be a punk or a biker. But I still didn't realise the stigma that was attached to Samaritans as hated people who were not part of the Jewish race. The thought that a Samaritan could help someone would be completely offensive to the people of Jesus' time. A similarity can be drawn to the woman at the well in John 4. Not only was she a Samaritan, but she was also a woman, and possibly a woman of 'dubious character'. Jesus was being radical to even talk to this person, let alone meet her and ask her for a drink. But somehow over the years we have made these things appear sterile; we've made them polite and nice. And as John Eldredge talks about in his book *Wild at Heart*, we've made the pinnacle of Christian manhood to become a 'nice guy'. 'Nice' is probably one of the most over-used and, to me, offensive words in the dictionary, because it removes power from people.

'Don't take the path of humility because you are trying to be nice or to please people. Don't walk in simpering weakness. Choose to lay down your strength and serve.' (John Eldredge)

I have a reputation among my friends for speaking my mind. I try to do it as appropriately as I can, but just occasionally I want to speak my *full* mind rather than keep things to myself. And this continues into all areas of my life, including shopping. I believe if we're not happy with products, or if they're faulty, then we should complain! Let's take them back to the shop. Do it in the right balanced way, but actually get the justice that we deserve. It seems that a lot of Christians just don't complain, because they would rather be 'nice'.

I remember on our wedding night we had a room at Manchester airport hotel before we were due to fly to New York the next day. As you can imagine this night was something I had looked forward to . . . for the whole of my life! We were given our room number and travelled what seemed like a mile down endless characterless corridors to find our room. We got there and I picked up Clare to carry her across the threshold, when we opened the door and saw to our horror what every bride and groom were not expecting to see . . . two single beds! So without a pause I said to Clare, 'Right, you wait there!' I ran to the reception area and told them *in no uncertain terms* that I was about to exercise my new freedom and I could not do that in a single bed! They obviously saw the severity of the situation and rectified it immediately! The story stops here!

The best way to avoid becoming a constant moaner, of course, is to tell people when you are happy as well. I thanked a waitress once for her excellent service, and she didn't know what to do – it was hilarious!

Humble pie

Recently at Leeds Faith In Schools, I've been involved in the whole fundraising process by writing to trusts, businesses and local churches to secure our future through raising money. One of the first things I realised, as I started on this venture, is that I must get rid of false humility: 'Oh, they won't give us any money; surely we're not worth it; we're only a little project . . .' But actually when you're fundraising you have to say that you *are* doing a good job, and you *are* worth the contribution you're requesting.

In my travels with my band HOG, I spent a lot of time with gifted musicians, and for a while it wasn't very fashionable to take on the praise that people gave you. The correct answer would be, 'Give the glory to the Lord, not me . . .' Now, when someone says I'm a good DJ, I do give glory to God because he gave me the gift, but I also say 'Thanks a lot', because it makes me feel good to know I am a pretty good DJ! I'm not the best, and I'm not going to show off about it, but I welcome encouragement. That's very different from just pointing to the sky and saying it's just the Lord's glory. If you're a good guitarist, or a good businessman, then let people say it, and let's take on real compliments to make the world slightly more realistic, especially in the church!

Of course, if you don't hold your tongue all the time, it

may appear that you are slightly rude. Often, it's not rudeness, just boldness in telling the truth. I wonder how many church members have got more equipment than they need or can afford, simply because they're too embarrassed to ask to borrow it? If we need a lawnmower, I'll ask my neighbour and he'll lend me one; then we'll lend him our hedgetrimmers. And actually in churches and neighbourhoods, that is how we need to be. In doing this we actually see more of each other and become more of a community. It's just that we need to have the guts to say, 'I need this, can you help me?'

'Most English people's goal in life is to get to the grave without ever being embarrassed.' (John Cleese)

This is particularly relevant in fundraising, where as a youth work organisation we need lots of equipment, computers, video projector, etc. I've found that being very specific with people is helpful. So writing to organisations and saying, 'I need this from you; can you give it to me?' is much more helpful than, 'Please can you help me?' Let's not be over polite, and maybe we can get the things that we need to do God's work more effectively.

I spent my teenage years cringing at Christian events because of the various T-shirts that were around. Thankfully there are some great Christian T-shirt manufacturers and design houses now, but in the time when I was growing up it was literally pictures of cute turtles and butterflies with comments which implied 'Jesus is very nice indeed'. For a teenage lad growing up, those T-shirts and sweatshirts couldn't have been any further from the person that I was and the tastes that I had as a DJ. I was trying to find a voice in the Christian world to express the gifts that I had, and cute turtles had nothing to do with it!

God isn't 'nice' to us. He loves us and he likes us, but he's not a 'nice' person, because a 'nice' person wouldn't actually discipline us, wouldn't actually make us fit to run the race. The grace of God is not being nice. The grace of God is undeserved favour. If God were just nice, he wouldn't give us the Holy Spirit to prod us and change our attitudes, to push us in deeper with him, and to convict us of sin. I'm just thankful that God loves me and likes me, but is willing to challenge me.

The following story is taken from the verbatim accounts of Smith Wigglesworth from the Assemblies of God archives of a visit to Belfast in 1926.

> One day at 11 o'clock I saw a woman with a tumour. She could live out one day. I said, 'Do you want to live?' She could not speak. She just moved her finger . . . I said, 'In the name of Jesus,' and I poured on the oil. The doctor said, 'She's gone.' A little blind girl led me to the bedside. Compassion broke me up for the child's sake . . . carrying the mother across the room I put her up against the wardrobe. I held her there. I said, 'In the name of Jesus death come out!' Like a fallen tree, leaf after leaf, her body began moving – upright instead of lifeless. Her feet touched the floor. 'In Jesus' name walk!' I said, and she did, back to bed. There was a doctor there, sceptical. He saw her. She said, 'I was in heaven, countless numbers, all like Jesus.' He pointed and I knew I had to go.

Smith appeared to have grabbed this dead woman, pushed her against the wardrobe and shouted at her to live! That wasn't very polite was it?

Questions

1. What makes you most embarrassed?
2. Read and discuss Luke chapter 19. How would you have reacted to this situation?
3. What is false humility?
4. What makes you hold back what you think?

16
The Career Magnet

LEE JACKSON

'When I was a boy of 14, my father was so ignorant, I could hardly stand to have the old man around. When I got to be 21, I was astonished at how much the old man had learned in seven years.' (Mark Twain)

It's true that most of us think that our dads don't understand much as we're growing up, but there are a few things I remember my dad telling me as we discussed life, the universe, and everything. One of the things he told me was that Christians are always radical until they have 'their button pushed by God'. Full on, born again, singing and dancing, radical Christians, may sink back for several reasons, the main ones being money, status, family and career. The 'career-magnet' has amazing power over men; it will soon take over if given half a chance.

I believe that every single one of us lives by faith whether we have a lot of money or whether we have no money at all. But somehow, when someone has a job which pays bills very well, and becomes a 'career', they can seem to lose their faith in God and place more faith in their job. Their whole being, existence, status, self-esteem, and self-image are all connected to their job. This is a scary prospect, especially when they say we are all two pay cheques away from the homeless shelter. I suppose we should ask, 'Where is our security?' Is our security in work? Or is it in God?

'You are not your job.' (From the film *Fight Club*)

The world of work is changing rapidly. When I was a civil servant – before most of it became privatised agencies – it was literally a job for life, and I worked with people who had been there for 40 years or more and who were just waiting for retirement – they were 'unsackable'. They knew the system well and did just enough to scrape by, while making the rest of us miserable! I got so fed up with the moaning of one colleague one day that I said to her, 'Why don't you just leave!' I felt like a stranger walking into a Wild West saloon! I am sure I saw tumbleweed going past the door! Now the world of work has changed. People are often under threat of redundancy on a monthly basis. They have short-term contracts, or are consultants or contractors, so work for small periods of time always hoping that the contract will be renewed again. This really puts the pressure on Christians to question where their security lies. Yosser Hughes from the gritty eighties drama *The Boys from the Black Stuff* was a symbol of how a job is often the man.

The threat of redundancy is, I believe, one of the things that really strikes fear deep into men's hearts especially if they have a family, or need to support a large house or an expensive car. It's as if their whole life is on the line.

Please don't misunderstand me – I'm not into so-called 'Christian' and 'non-Christian' jobs, I just believe there are different ways to serve God. Some people really do serve God well in their chosen career. My friends John and Fiona are both career-minded people, and it's interesting to hear their struggles and anxieties as we pray that they would be followers of Jesus in their work environment.

I find it difficult as well when young people don't want to serve God, or usually more often are not *allowed* to serve God for short-term mission or training. I've seen some excellent Christian young people whose parents have put enormous pressure on them not to take a 'year out', because they want their children to get a 'decent' job. In this way, parents teach their kids that serving God isn't a proper job – no wonder we are in a mess! Of course it is much harder now for a graduate to take a year out because there are so many debts to pay off! Catch 22.

Most parents ask their children, 'What are you going to do when you grow up?' Something with status is always desirable, such as a doctor or solicitor, especially in middle-class environments, which is, frankly, most of the church in the UK.

'Fathers send their children to college either because they went to college, or because they did not.' (L. L. Hendren)

One of the other issues not talked about much is 'hiding' in your job. I've certainly been tempted and guilty of this myself. A good friend of mine who is a manager and deals with overtime is absolutely convinced that some of the men who work for her deliberately take overtime so they don't have to spend time with their families. If they don't want to attend something – a family gathering or event – that is when they'll say, 'Sorry, I'm working.' If you say, 'Actually, I quite fancy staying at home,' or 'I'm seeing my wife tonight,' then people will question you, but not if you say you are working! Some men hide from their families, from real relationships, and they use their jobs as a place where they don't have to be Dad and they don't have to be sharing the TV remote control with somebody else!

I think we have to ask ourselves – do we do this? Have we been guilty of hiding in our jobs in the past? Are we doing that now? Do we work longer than we have to? I could busy myself in my job and keep myself there all night if I wanted to, but actually those things aren't so important that I would miss seeing my kids before they go to bed. It's amazing the games we play with ourselves, in our minds and with our families, and how easily we can use our jobs to hide from things we don't want to face. This is often seen in so-called ministry, as of course leading a church or mission organisation is an endless task!

'Remember if you win the rat race – you are still a rat!' (Anon)

I once played basketball with a guy who worked seven days a week, and he was the most miserable man I had ever met. I think he actually enjoyed it in a strange sort of way! Of course there are financial pressures, but actually taking a day off will help us to do our jobs better in the other five or six days. I know for myself that after a while at work I may be there but I'm not really doing the job very well, and I believe Jesus asks us to do everything to the best of our ability.

'Unless the job means more than the pay, it will never pay more.' (H. Bertram Lewis)

The financial decisions we make can become a trap. We get a good job, we buy a big house, we get a better car, and we make the decision sometimes to send our kids to private school. This can then affect the rest of our lives because we feel we have to keep the kids in that school, we have to keep a house that size, and we need to have a big car, etc. And those things become the excuse that drives us to the catch 22 situation that often distorted careers can bring. Being a Christian, as you know, is just simply following Jesus, and in following him we have to talk to him and ask him what he wants. As we become more like him, we don't need to spend hours in prayer trying to make a small decision, because we know what he would think about it. The financial decisions we make, often done in good heart, do have repercussions on our priorities, and if we're not very careful can drive us away from being Christ-like in all aspects. These are the practical things that Jesus is interested in – how we live out life, and how we actually follow him. I know most men's desire is to provide for their family, and I believe that's a good thing and the right thing, but we must have God in the equation. We can't do it alone.

Clare and I are often short of money because we don't bring much in, and being a DJ and having twins puts a lot of pressure on us financially. I believe I'm taking a more practical view on lots of things now. Just the other week I did some extra basketball coaching for the council, which paid quite well, and that was a good use of my time, but I also need to have my faith mixed into that. I need to pray that God will provide the things that we need, as well as doing things practically for myself. Some people are called to live by faith completely, which means relying on God for everything with no income. Others – like me – are made to work and have faith as well. It's about finding the balance and finding our trust in God through the whole thing.

'The things you own, end up owning you.' (From the film *Fight Club*)

I spoke to a guy called Douglas at a conference recently and he actually had everything that he wanted. He could have followed in his father's footsteps in a multimillion pound business. He had a mobile when no one else had one, a sports car, all the women that he wanted, everything materially that he wanted, but he said he got to a point where he was suddenly aware that he really needed God. Even though in the world's eyes he wanted for nothing, he still had an enormous desire and massive need for God. So the whole idea of how our life would be sorted out if we won the lottery is a lie, because unless we submit our careers and our lives wholly to God then we will never truly follow our heart, and we will never really be living. Douglas said he had to leave his job to live in a run-down house with a few lads who were on fire for Jesus before he started to live. God sorted him out and also brought him the woman that will continue to sort him out! As we talked we agreed that actually materialism is nothing to do with how much money you've got; it's an attitude of heart. You can be living on benefits and be extremely materialistic, or you can have a million pounds and not be.

Being busy is not necessarily a sign of success. A friend of mine taught me a lesson in how to live my life. Paul is a real success in the world's eyes – a single young dentist, and popular with the ladies. But as I talked to him about his work I realised he has made some great decisions. He works just four days a week, and he chooses not to do the work that just brings in the most money – he likes to meet real people. He has a balanced life and has made godly decisions even though he is not a Christian! He seems more sorted than a lot of Christians I know!

Maybe we fall into easy, safe career options, because we don't actually believe that training for ministry is a 'proper job'. However, I believe the role of full-time ministry also needs to be challenged regularly to make sure that we're not using it as a reason not to live in the real world. If we're going to stand up as radical men, we need to challenge ourselves and each other regularly.

'Don't become so well-adjusted to your culture that you fit into it without even thinking. Instead, fix your attention on God.' (Romans 12:2 *The Message*)

Questions

1. Do we put too much value on being busy?
2. What is a 'proper job'?
3. Is there a difference between a job and a career?
4. Do you hide in your job?
5. What cultural aspects of work put pressure on you in the light of Romans 12:2?
6. What would happen if you were made redundant?

EBB AND FLOW

The Celtic Christians had an amazing understanding of God's creation and would often talk about the flow of the tides as their philosophy on living their lives.

The worldview of the Celts was remarkably holistic . . . passionate, adventurous and full of wandering, their Eastern influenced spirituality also gave them a great appetite for meditation, Scripture and seeking God. It is this unique spiritual 'genetic code', reflected in our aboriginal apostles, which resonates so strongly with us today. (Roger Ellis and Chris Seaton, *New Celts*, Kingsway Publications)

On Lindisfarne, now known as Holy Island, (the place where indigenous Christianity started in Britain) one of my favourite places is Cuthbert's island, which is a few hundred yards off the beach and only accessible for a few hours a day. St Cuthbert was a great character – he once spent the night waist deep in the sea in order to stay awake to pray! He used to go there because he knew he needed uninterrupted time with God. When the tide was in he could not get back to land; it was just him, his lantern and God.

Cuthbert, very like tidal Holy Island, recognised the need for rhythm in life. It cannot be all open, or all closed. Life needs a balance. Sometimes we need to be very much part of the mainland and all that is going on; at other times we need to be an island for a while. We all need space, a time set apart, free from noise and busyness. If we cannot find an island we need to create one. Perpetual busyness is a great danger to the life of the spirit. (David Adam, *The Pilgrims Guide*, Canterbury Press)

- Do we need a sense of the ebb and flow of the tides in our life?
- How does technology help or hinder us in this quest?
- Why do people burn out?
- Do you know people who need to slow down?
- If we keep pushing what happens?
- What did Jesus teach us of the ebb and flow?

17

The Doorway to the Kingdom is Three Feet High

JOHN O'BRIEN

I'm afraid during my not-yet Christian days at school, I showed little respect and time for any members of staff. If I could find ways to mimic, humiliate and make their day an unproductive one, I would give myself a little tick next to my name with the phrase 'Tried his best, well done!'. Thinking about most of my teachers from back then, they just blur together now. I can't squeeze out a fond memory in favour of any of them. Apart from one – Dave Bradley.

Over the years, I have become a little more emotionally mature. I've come to realise what I couldn't verbalise back then – that I loved Dave Bradley. Now before you throw this book down, spit in disgust and pray for my sexuality, read on. Whether it was because I never had a father, or because I suffered verbal and emotional abuse from my stepfather, who knows?

Dave Bradley was our drama teacher. It goes without saying that because of his passion and skill for the dramatic, it was only a matter of time before I loved his lessons, and later on left school with two qualifications, one of them being in drama. Why did I love him? Because I didn't see him as a teacher. I grew over the years to like Dave Bradley, and then to respect and inevitably love him. There were four of us altogether who felt this way. I would have done anything he asked; in fact on more than one occasion I did. One of the perks of drama lessons was being able to wear jeans as opposed to formal trousers. My drama lesson would be last period of the day, but I would wear my jeans in anticipation from lunchtime onwards, which was of course not school policy. I remember teachers trying in vain to get me to change, but I would cunningly refuse to worm out of my Wranglers. Then Dave Bradley sidled up to me and very gently and lovingly explained that he'd heard I was being disobedient. I was devastated, not because I had been exposed, but because I feared he may have been disappointed in me and our friendship threatened. So what was I to do? It was simple. I wore my formal trousers. Why? Mr Bradley wasn't a 'teacher'; he was a man who loved his craft, who loved the many varied methods of training me in it, and who loved me. Of course I would obey him – wouldn't you?

I remember him taking the four of us to one side during our final week at school and telling us with a calm authority that we had what it took to become actors. Then with loving honesty and sincerity in his eyes he explained how unstable and inconsistent it might be to get work. I knew he had my best interest at heart – I could see it. My last thrilling time with Mr Bradley was in the following winter after leaving school. Four of us were invited to spend the day with him, his wife and black labrador. We went out for walks and had snowball fights and, after dark, as he escorted us to the train, it began to snow heavily. I remember praying desperately that it would be so deep that we would have to stay over, just so we could enjoy his company some more. I missed him so much in those early years. I wish I had stayed in touch.

Today I have a wonderful wife and two God-given boys. The saying is true that you never forget a good teacher, and I have never forgotten Mr Bradley. I sometimes imagine welcoming him into my home and proudly showing off my family and telling him what an impact he had on my life. I would mention all the benefits of knowing him: the unspoken gestures, lifestyle, attitudes, his smile, the spoken words of encouragement, his laugh. I would say, 'Dave, I want you to know that you were the first to make an impact on my life, and all the invisible qualities that you maybe unknowingly tumbled into my life, in a funny sort of way, have become gems somewhere in my spirit reflected in the lives of my children. I love them and I have made it my aim to tell them that fact every day of their lives. Thank you.' Then I would have hugged him.

By the way, just in case you were wondering, because I saw it in Dave's eyes that day at the tender age of 15, I took his advice and never pursued acting professionally. The Lord used this man to shape my destiny.

For the children's sake

Many years later, three of us arrived in Latvia a little uncertain of all the details of our trip. My good friends and children's ministers, Graham and Steph Reed, and myself knew our main area of ministry would be to train these beautiful Latvian people each evening for about two hours on a variety of issues relating to working with children. But no one told us about Friday! Friday lasted 14 hours, with non-stop teaching, training and talking. Thrown into the middle of the day was a two-and-a-half hour event with a group of street children. They were captivated by the lively songs, speechless during the storytelling and laughed all the way through the parachute games played with an old blanket.

Smelly and totally dishevelled, they stood quietly by us with their eyes open but the lights out.

At the end of our time, we offered prayer for any child who needed to know God's love. Children came forward to receive any love we had to give. We prayed with a brother and sister both under twelve years old. Smelly and totally dishevelled, they stood quietly by us with their eyes open but the lights out. I prayed that the Lord might touch them. The boy's face still looked lifeless as two huge tears rolled down his cheeks. I knew the procedure; I knew how to be politically correct and safe. I knew the rules: look but do not touch, love from a distance. I took the boy in my arms and held on to him for what seemed an eternity. I prayed, hugged and willed that this child would experience something he never knew – love.

When we prayed with a young girl, she calmly announced that she did have somewhere to live but her father beat her. Last time she was thrown out and had to live on the streets for a month, after which she was allowed home. She was only nine years old. The same rules were broken. We embraced her and later, when the children had left, we ourselves cried.

In the first eleven verses of Matthew 19, we read how the men and women came to muscle in on Jesus' time and power. Many were healed and set free. Then the Pharisees tested him with their verbal theological diarrhoea, and failed as usual to catch him out. Now it was the time for the children. They had been waiting in the wings for the host of the party to be available to give them some quality time. Maybe Jesus had healed some of their parents. As they drew closer, they knew here was a man unlike any other; no proud look of a Pharisee, no suspicious glare of a soldier, no hopeless glance of a weary father, but a look of a man with power, love and self-control, who spoke, taught and did amazing things.

Children need to be around men like this. The sparkle of joy in the eyes of the children soon turned to hurt and disappointment when the hands of the disciples barred the way through to Jesus. Some began to cry, out of sadness of not being allowed to spend a few precious moments with the hero of the universe. Their loss lasted only a moment, for a strong voice called out, and the children swung around to see Jesus' arms outstretched: 'Let the little children come to me.' They ran, faces beaming to the side of Jesus. 'Don't ever stop children coming to me'. Embracing them, ruffling their hair, laughing, 'For the kingdom of heaven belongs to such as these.'

Then the touch. The creator of life placed his hands on them. Scripture doesn't tell us that power left him, but at the very least a blessing would have been passed on to the expectant children. Then, with Jesus' ministry complete for that moment, he left. Imagine years later when the early church had begun, the buzzing excitement of believers talking about their memories of Jesus, and one young man sharing: 'For me it happened when as a boy Jesus welcomed me. He spent time with me and placed his hands on my head, and as he looked peacefully into my eyes I knew this was no ordinary man. He cared for me and gave me permission back then as a child to love, follow and obey him. That's why I'm where I am today.'

If you are a man, young or old, then I would encourage you, urge you, to begin to make a difference in the lives of children around you, at home, in your church, among your friends. 'Oh Lord, I want to live my life for you in this generation. I want to make a difference with your help, Lord. Fill me up with your life, passion, power and anointing so I can, at the very least, reflect your life to children, and at the very most excite, empower and equip them to be radical followers of Jesus.'

It only takes one person to make a difference – will that be you? If God has done it before, guess what? He can do it again. I ask myself what I am leaving behind for my own children and those I meet every day. I want every encounter to be one that will make a difference. What a testimony it would be if years later, when I'm out of here, for at least one person to say because of me they are following Jesus, living for him and doing what he did.

Be a mentor

In the *Concise Oxford Dictionary* the definition of the word 'mentor' reads, 'Experienced and trusted adviser'. In the course of my ministry, I have had the privilege to mentor several children and young people; young lives that have asked me to get alongside them for counsel, advice, prayer and with their permission to ask those straightforward questions which would help guide them in their walk with Jesus. 'How is your prayer life? What issues of personality, family, sexuality are you struggling with? How are you dealing with any sin issues? How are you keeping short accounts with Jesus?' And other light and humorous topics! This is a good way of relating to children. Don't worry if, like me, you are not up on the latest music, fashion, gossip, games, films, soaps, etc. What children really want, even in all that the world offers, is relationship. Mentoring is one useful means of creating that. I suggest no more than two or three people to mentor at any one time. Remember to be vulnerable yourself, because growth and depth will develop in your relationship if you are also open and honest about your weaknesses and failures.

Releasing children

We need to hold on lightly to our children when it comes to their service and calling for the Lord.

I love it when Aslan, the great lion of Narnia, speaks directly to King Peter and Queen Susan, and then later to Edmund and Lucy. With a serious tone in his commanding voice, he breaks the sad news that they will no longer be returning to Narnia because they are too old! Barely in their teens they are told that their service has now been completed. How often do we tell our children to wait? Wait until you are older. Wait until you have the know-how. We need to hold on lightly to our children when it comes to their service and calling for the Lord.

Scripture gives us fascinating accounts of God using children in his service as prophets (the boy Samuel, 1 Samuel 3:1) and kings (young David, 1 Samuel 18:2). Just these two boys, for example, were released from the care and training of their mentors to pursue the plans of God.

Often, in my travels, I take a small group of children and youth to help minister during our children's missions. This has two advantages. First, it gives them an opportunity to serve the Lord practically, thus growing in experience and confidence. Second, it can help those who are sounding out a calling on their lives to serve the Lord full time; to identify their areas of gifting and anointing while building character and personality at the same time.

When I spoke to William, he was helping in the ministry at a men's workshop I was attending. He gave his testimony and shared words from the Lord to other men also present. He told me that during the week he runs a business and oversees his staff, and frequently travels to his other European office in France to head up the team. William is 17 years old.

The heart of a revivalist

She had every right to hold back the crucial information, which would have brought freedom and healing to this sick but valiant soldier. The young girl had been taken captive, seized from her beloved homeland, and forced to work as a slave for the wife whose husband, as chief of the king's army, was responsible for her predicament. This girl was from Israel. She loved God. In the end she decided to speak out the words that would lead to the commander's cure and perhaps, at the very least, a mini revival in the household and neighbourhood of this great soldier.

I would encourage you to read the account for yourself, and with God's help, draw your own conclusions. You can find the story in 2 Kings 5 verses 1 to 19.

Others have written fine books concerning children and revival, and it is well documented how the Lord has used children to do great things throughout history. If this is an area of potential passion for you then get hold of what you can! All I would add is this, Jesus loves children and heaven will be teeming with them: young warriors who have answered his call to live in a radical pursuit of him and put his kingdom and all that he requires first. In Matthew 18 verses 1 to 14, Jesus tells the blushing, platform-seeking, and status-striving disciples a thing or two about who really is the greatest in the kingdom of heaven. I've already been accused of saying that children are more important than adults. What I want to be held accountable for is this: the Lord is still wanting childlike, humble, Jesus face-seeking hearts to do his will, whether young or old.

Jesus and children

I do believe wholeheartedly in child evangelism and conversion. Just recently my wife and I had a God-given moment, which lasted for about 20 minutes, debating the topic of heaven and hell brought up by our six- and four-year-olds. Even at that age they have the will and power to make a decision whether they want to love the Lord and follow him or not. Since the day our children entered God's creation, we as parents have never had to teach our children to be naughty. That was an inheritance they received at birth. Since then, we have constantly tried to train them to do what's right.

So, in your own pursuit of a fulfilling, vibrant relationship with Jesus, don't forget to keep your eyes open for those children who love the Lord and have his hand on their lives, who want to move in the things of God. Start with those who want to pursue him. It is always easier to move an object forward that wants to be moved! The Lord will encourage those who don't.

To silence the foe and the avenger

Sam was the youngest member, at five years old, sitting with his mum at the back of the room of 30 children attending an hour's seminar I was teaching entitled 'You can live for Jesus'. At the end, during a ministry time, Sam, holding his mother's hand, led her out to the front to see me. He told me that he had been hearing God's voice at home for some time and wondered if it was related to his mum. I discovered that Sam's mum had reluctantly agreed to go on an Alpha course and had made it quite clear that if she attended it would not make any difference, mainly because of the occult involvement in her life. Talking to her afterwards, she told me she had effectively banned God in all areas from her home, through books, media and conversation. No one had told Sam that. Sam would speak out what the Lord wanted her to hear. Mum was gobsmacked! Maybe there was something in this. So, as a result of her five-year-old son and other God-incidences, she gave her life to Jesus. As part of her testimony at church she came in holding a plastic bag full of the ashes from books on the occult and other materials that she had burned very early that morning, one of the books being the first she received at the age of eight which started her unhappy journey into this lifestyle. Several items outstanding were handed over to her elders, namely two crystal balls and a pagan knife. So outside with a sledgehammer in tow they smashed the last hold of her old life into pieces. The word of the Lord brought the joy of the Lord through a small boy aged five.

Sam's sister picked up a ring that the Lord had told her mum to remove. It was fashioned into a pentagram (a five-pointed star) and had previously been used in occult practices. It was left on her dresser and her mum had tried in vain to squash the ring herself, but Sam's sister, with the ring in her two fingers, squashed it flat. Not bad for a two-and-a-half-year-old.

A mandate from the Lord

When I visited my son's school to lead the infant Christmas assembly, one girl was obviously captivated by hearing the nativity story. When the children began to file out, she broke rank and walked over to me. I can remember how she looked. Her eyes puzzled, and with a frown on her forehead, she asked in such a questioning tone, 'Why was Jesus so special?' My mouth fumbled for the right answer. 'Because he is the Son of God,' I said. Moments later the hall was empty. As I walked home I felt led to intercede for her, praying that the word of truth would be planted in her heart and this would be the beginning of a remarkable discovery of Jesus for herself.

2 Corinthians 4 verse 4 says, 'The god of this age has blinded the minds of unbelievers, so that they cannot see the light of the gospel of the glory of Christ, who is the image of God.' I believe we have a mandate from the Lord, a command and a commission from the captain of the armies of heaven, Jesus himself, laid down to us in the first eight verses of Psalm 78. Man of God, whoever you are, whatever your profession and calling, I stand with you and

ask the Lord to help us both. The writer of Psalm 78 seems to arise from a verbal slumber and with the clearing of his throat effectively says, 'It's about time I put the record straight, I will remain silent no longer. I will open my mouth, I will utter hidden things, things from of old. I have heard and known the cracking good news of our great God told to us by our fathers, passed down to us by the men of God who were not afraid.' Then the writer really starts to pace the platform in verse 4, 'We will not hide them from their children; we will tell the next generation the praiseworthy deeds of the Lord, his power and the wonders he has done.' No longer should we let the voice of our enemy dictate and enslave this generation of children. I have never before experienced such an intensity of open spiritual abuse of a demonic nature on our children. Our tolerance level has been diluted, so we say it is OK for our children to ride broomsticks, cast spells and chase vampires.

I saw an advert in the travel section of a paper recently entitled 'Wizard camp'. A week's holiday for nine- to twelve-year-olds exploring what? God-centred values? I don't think so. You can buy for the princely sum of £22 a children's book of spells from a reputable book shop. Let us stand up for what is right and dare to be different at this time. A small window in a darkened room can still pour in substantial light over the lives of many children in the UK.

Romans 16 verse 19 reads, 'I want you to be wise about what is good, and innocent about what is evil'. Psalm 78 verse 4 urges us to come on! Now is the time to lift Jesus above the enemy; to dare to speak out about what is not right.

Verse 5 of Psalm 78 continues, '. . . to teach their children, so that the next generation would know . . . and put their trust in God.' We are in danger of the next generation not having a clue concerning who God is. During a fun quiz with a hall full of juniors I asked them questions about the Christmas story. I asked what were the three gifts the wise men brought to Jesus. Three separate children answered wood, pyjamas and champagne. They were not joking. That was seven years ago. What would they answer today?

Psalm 78 continues with an abundance of miraculous accounts of the birthing and growth of God's people. What will be the result of us selling our souls for this mandate? A new generation of children who (verse 7) 'will put their trust in God', turn from the destructive 'toys' of the enemy to living with the tools of God's anointing, and follow his instructions so the next generation will know them.

Father, I pray that men will change so that their hearts will be loyal to you, and their spirits will remain faithful to you alone. Amen and amen.

Let me end this chapter with a story. P.U.S.H. (Pray Until Something Happens) was a large gathering of people, who, from 2 pm until 10 pm one cloudy Saturday in May met together in a prayer concert. The worship stirred us to pray for many issues and people groups in our city and across the UK. Steven had come with a group of friends. I was told a few days later that Steven was in awe of what he had experienced on that day. Maybe it was the dynamic, relevant and interactive programme or the quality of sound and musicianship of the artists, or it may have been that the prayer throughout the day was real, specific and most of the time in bite-sized chunks.

The next day Steven gave his life over to the Lord. He told his friends they were not to expect him in church or any meetings during that week. Why? Surely that would be the one place to receive support and encouragement? Steven announced that he would remain at home for that time, because he wanted his family to see that there was a change in his life. He is eleven.

If you want to move forward in the things mentioned in this chapter, but you are aware of past hindrances, hurts and failures, then take some moments to allow the Lord to reveal specific issues to you. Seek forgiveness and forgive others if appropriate; ask the Lord to cleanse, empower and direct you.

Questions

1. In what ways, with your gifting and strengths, can you get alongside children? Ask the Lord to show you.
2. Is there someone you could begin to mentor? In conjunction with a parent or children's leader, discuss which child has 'the hand of the Lord' on them.
3. Are you 'holding on' to that child lightly?
4. What can you do to fulfil a little of Psalm 78 verses 1 to 8?

CHRISTIAN GHETTO

Let's get out and take an expression of community built on the foundation of true biblical love to the world around us. No more them and us!

It's not OK for us to choose what we decide to surrender to God – it must be our whole life. To daily pick up our cross and daily die to self. Living sacrifices. Let's not try and crawl under the table.

(Caleb)

18

The False Divide

Lee Jackson

One of the things that has fascinated me over my 20 plus years in the church in the UK has been the number of things in church culture that are taught as if they are in the Bible when really they are not. One example is the great chasm that is supposed to exist in society between the sacred and the secular.

I was one of the first Christian DJs, and it was a little bit of a novelty for a while. No one had ever seen a DJ in a gig before in the early nineties especially in Christian worship events, and I used to use a lot of material which came out on Christian record labels. Some of it was very good, like Hydro and all the radical club music which came out at the time, dripping with the Holy Spirit – but I soon realised there was actually very little high quality Christian dance music. So I used to just play whatever 'secular' music I liked, and people still come up to me today and say, 'Where do you get all your Christian dance music from?'. I pick records off the shelf that I like the look of, I pray, and then listen to the music and decide whether or not to buy them.

There is nothing more to it than that and I don't fast before I buy. I have got a nose for a good or bad tune and the rest is common sense (or maybe a bit of discernment if you want to spiritualise it!).

'The only truly secular thing is sin.' (Roger Ellis, *New Celts*)

The simple truth is there is really no such thing as 'Christian' and 'secular'. The Bible makes no distinctions between the two. I say to people quite simply that there's good and there's bad music, helpful music, and not very helpful, and neutral music. 'Everything is permissible – but not everything is beneficial.' (1 Corinthians 10:23) I've had a few arguments with people about this over the years and the length that people go to is quite fascinating. How can an instrumental piece of music be Christian or non-Christian? A lot of dance music is instrumental, and it's useful sometimes to have no words and just allow people to dance and reach God through what's happening. People go to ridiculous lengths to try and prove that secular music is dangerous, and really the argument goes nowhere. They say, 'Well, maybe it's the samples they use in the track', or 'Maybe it's the drums.' But the fact is that most drum samples are made in a studio by a technician, and if you use a one-second drum sample recorded for Yamaha it doesn't mean that it's not 'Christian music' you're creating. My friend Kenny (who's a DJ in New York) simply says, 'Is your car Christian or non-Christian?' People answer, 'Well, it's just my car . . .', and he says, 'Well, it's just my music . . .' And it's as simple as that! If we can get rid of this false divide, then I believe that Christians will impact society in a much more meaningful way.

Guerrilla warfare

Christians have made attempts on the charts over the years, trying to get into the Top 40. They want to get out there, get a Christian song in the charts and make a small impact with the three minutes' play in the Top-40 run down. But actually this propagates the sacred / secular divide. I respect people like Delirious? (who have taken a lot of criticism from Christians). I just love their attitude that they are not Christians who are trying to get into the charts, but they are a good band who happen to be Christians. They make good music, and they do want to chart – but also, they want to impact the whole music scene. I remember Martin Smith saying once that he wants to meet Liam Gallagher and speak to him about Jesus in a natural way, and I really believe that he does want to do that. It's not the way other bands operate – run out of the bushes, throw a few holy song hand-grenades, and then run back into the safety of their nice Christian ghetto. We need to get an understanding of how God wants us to live in society where there's a blurring of the boundaries between the sacred and secular. Real evangelism happens in youth groups where Christians and non-Christians interact together normally.

Some people are actually scared of 'contamination' especially when it comes to young people. As a youth worker I have had conversations with well-meaning Christian parents around the issue of contamination by the big bad world. Yes, the world does have major problems, and things that will tempt us, and some people will fall. But what we need to do is train ourselves fully for the battle – discipline ourselves so that we can live in society *and* still be a credible witness. But most importantly *stay* in society, and not get into the guerrilla warfare mentality.

I was at a wedding recently, and it was one of those full-day jobs which went on to the early hours of the morning. It was great to meet some of my old friends and find out what had been happening in their lives. (And it was sad in many ways to see what had not been happening in their lives.) We were staying in the hotel without the kids, and didn't have to drive anywhere, so I had a drink and just took things easy (I'm not even going to enter into the discussion on whether Christians should drink or not – that's completely up to you!). Personally I quite enjoy relaxing with my friends and a beer!

What happened at the wedding was that as the evening went on people got steadily more and more drunk, which is always sad to watch, but I was taking it steady and was quite happy just to relax with them. Maybe I winced at one or two of the jokes now and again, but I was happy to be in that culture trying to be holy. Jesus went to parties and was holy in some very difficult places indeed, even with people who were out to kill him. In biblical times, a wedding was probably more than a one-day event, and I'm sure people got very drunk, but Jesus remained holy in these hard places and I think we need to follow that model where we can.

John Drane (head of practical theology at the University of Aberdeen) went to a New Age fair and set up a stall called The Secret of the Tarot. He did some research into tarot cards and found out that most are of biblical symbols, scenes and people, so what he did was allow people to come to his stall, show them the cards, and explain to them what the cards *actually* meant and how they pointed to Jesus. Now some people reading this will be putting pen to paper to complain, but I listened to this guy and I was fascinated that he didn't see the New Age movement as a threat, but as a great opportunity to talk about Jesus to people in society who are open spiritually. I was so excited to hear what a radical man he was, being salt and light in one of the most difficult environments possible. Of course, for most men, going into a brothel would not be a good idea, and they may not be salt and light in that situation! We must use our discernment in these things, as John Drane did. He was wise and radical – a great combination.

Sink or swim

Maybe our discipleship techniques need to be looked at. I've been so excited to see some radical youth groups discipling young people to live in the world. It's like learning to swim – some people learn to swim in a swimming pool, which is great, but once you start swimming in the ocean, it's a completely different environment, because the sea is real and the swimming pool isn't. Maybe our discipleship goes as far as teaching people to swim well in the swimming pool, but not against strong currents and against waves in the ocean. Over the last few years I've seen friends of mine I thought could swim well, but who have drowned in the culture of the world and are not following Jesus any more, which has been a great sadness to me.

You choose

I have been tempted in many different ways, and I really believe that people can choose *not* to fall away from Jesus. People can talk about it, they can theologise it, or whatever they want, but actually it's a choice. Are you choosing to fall away from Jesus? It's about knowing your boundaries; knowing how far you can handle things. I think it's obvious that we do have to run away from things sometimes, but other times we need to stop and to take captive our thoughts and our actions.

> The weapons we fight with are not the weapons of the world. On the contrary, they have divine power to demolish strongholds. We demolish arguments and every pretension that sets itself up against the knowledge of God, and we take captive every thought to make it obedient to Christ. (2 Corinthians 10:4–5)

Do you have an account?

There's been a lot of talk about accountability over the last few years. Some people don't really understand what it is, and I'm trying to learn myself. People are very happy to be 'accountable' until someone wants to hold them to account! When you're doing something wrong, and you're in an accountable relationship with someone you trust and admire, then that person needs to say, 'Well, actually that's out of order,' and you need to say, 'Yes, I understand that it's not right, and I will try not to do that again. Help me to do this.' That is what accountability is. It's not 'heavy shepherding', it's not heavy leadership – it's respecting somebody and allowing them to have input into your life, your temptations and your struggles. That's how we survive in the world. That's how we choose not to fall. A simple way to develop a real accountable relationship is to ask someone you respect, who is the same sex as you, to meet with you on a regular basis. Get them to ask you about the three main things you struggle with – it could be spending too much money, late night TV, or your relationship with your girlfriend or wife.

> This world is not your home, so don't make yourselves cosy in it. Don't indulge your ego at the expense of your soul. Live an exemplary life among the natives so that your actions will refute their prejudices. Then they'll be won over to God's side and be there to join in the celebration when he arrives. Make the Master proud of you by being good citizens. (1 Peter 2:11–13 *The Message*)

Nearly everywhere I go and speak, whether it's to men or not, I always say, 'you must have non-Christian friends', or people who are 'not yet Christians' (as they say now!). I'd go as far to say that if you don't have friends who are not Christians then you're probably not following Jesus as he means you to. Jesus certainly had friends who were not believers. We need to be party people.

> I am convinced that religion's historic concerns for dogma, orthodoxy, tradition, hierarchy, order and good taste are quite foreign to anything Jesus taught. He had deeper quests in mind, namely, touching the brokenhearted, healing the sick, welcoming the outcast, casting out demons, humbling the powerful, lifting up the lowly, feeding the hungry, releasing captives and giving sight to the blind. In pursuit of his quests, he brought people together and forged relationships. Our ritualised re-enactments of the Last Supper, whose every detail we have fought over and fine-tuned, fail to capture the radical and messy spirit of what Jesus himself did. My advice to pastors who dare to be effective: Throw lots of parties, get to know

> your flock, and then serve and preach to them as friends. Be ready for trouble, for when deepening relationships yield change, the agent of change will come under assault. My advice to lay leaders: Cut council meetings short, spend less time and heat on financial management, and instead bring food to the parties, embrace the new and overlooked, and protect the pastor when relationship-building bears the fruit of vitality and growth. My advice to evangelism teams: Skip the brochures, ads, telemarketing, follow-up cards and other easy stuff, and instead invite people to dinner. (Tom Ehrich, from the website www.biblicalrecorder.org)

We need to do what we can – have fun, tell jokes, dance (if you can!), but most of all let's be ourselves instead of grey-faced religious segregationists! Embarrass yourself occasionally! Have a laugh – it's OK – honest! That's how people will know that we are different.

> Living out this theology would empower and release inactive believers. There are millions who sense that the only way they can serve God is to sit there like good little church members and hope they make it into small group leadership! (Roger Ellis *New Celts*)

'The earth is the Lord's, and everything in it, the world, and all who live in it' (Psalm 24:1). The whole of the world belongs to God, although some of it is obviously corrupted because of the sinful nature of people and the fall of humankind. But doesn't that give us a great opportunity to actually be part of the world as active members instead of always complaining about it, making attacks into the enemy camp and then running back into the safety of our church worship and tea rotas?

Questions

1. What divides have you heard implied?
2. Is there anything that God cannot use for his purposes?
3. Are we scared of contamination?
4. How do we prevent guerrilla warfare?
5. How practical is being holy?
6. What are your experiences of accountable relationships?
7. Are you actually accountable to anyone? Do you need to be?
8. If we call something secular – are we saying that God cannot affect it? What does that do to God?

ACCOUNTABILITY

My advice to men would be about honest accountability – finding people that you can tell the truth to is the hardest thing in the world. Don't compromise in business, don't compromise on the football pitch, don't compromise in your church – just don't compromise!

- 'The balance between freedom and responsibility is a key for abundant life, find it with fun in your heart and accountability on your shoulder.'
- 'In my book every true evangelist has 60% non-christian friends.'
- 'Don't try to be a good Christian man, just be a good man who's a Christian.'
- 'He who dies with the most toys – still dies.'

(Jon)

19

The Fun Factory!

Andy Lenton

It all happened around 1990 when I got a position in a church in the north east of England. The church couldn't afford to pay any of my wages or expenses so I had to get a job, and at the time the unemployment rate was terrible. It even got to the stage where I asked the local window cleaner if he wanted a lad to carry his ladders. I was so distressed that I went to see my regional superintendent (church boss person) and he went through all the patronising patter about 'Have you tried to find a job? Where have you tried?', and so on. I told him the full extent of my efforts to try and get employment, and his eyes lit up when I mentioned the window cleaner. This was the last resort for me, but he said 'You get yourself a window cleaning round and I'll buy your ladders for you!' What an encouragement! Lisa and I were planning to get married at the time. I just cried my eyes out and said to her, 'If this is what the ministry is all about, don't get married to me – go and find somebody who can look after you.' I was really fed up.

But I decided that if that's what God wanted me to do

then I would do it, and lo and behold when I went back up to the north east the following week there was a letter through my door which said that I had an interview at a factory making lanse pipes for the steelworks. (These are massive ceramic pipes through which oxygen is blown, to withstand the intense high heat.) I went for the interview and got the job.

It was filthy work, and I used to come home every day looking like a coalman, covered in dust and grime and other terrible stuff. After a while at work I started coming out in incredible sores all the way up my arms and back, all across my torso, and down my legs. I went to the doctor to try and get this sorted out, and he sent me for tests. The tests at the hospital involved drawing a big grid on my back of about 48 different little squares and putting a different type of stuff on each square, to see if I was particularly allergic to anything. I had to keep this on for a week. I couldn't shower as it was stuck on by sticking plaster. It was very uncomfortable, and because I worked in such a filthy job, not being able to shower was a nightmare. After a week the only thing I was allergic to was the sticking plaster that they stuck the test on with! They eventually found out through my pinching stuff from work that some of the material we were working with was radioactive and the boss had never told us! The boss never found out that it was me that had taken the stuff, and he had to sort out his working practices, which was well overdue.

The lads who I worked with were typical north-easterners, plus one lad from Norwich. As time went on the lads did seem to like me, but when they found out I was a Christian and training for the ministry – well that was it. I was the butt of every joke and they tried every little thing to make me swear or look at a pornographic picture – that was their mission. I had to hide my sandwich box or it became a target. It started off with nuts and bolts in my sandwiches. Then it got steadily worse. Once I found a dead mouse in my lunch box, and then they started peeing in my sandwiches – it just got foul.

I thought if I laughed along with it they would pack it in eventually. I used to have to carry my tea mug around with me everywhere because they frequently peed in it and worse. This was pretty disgusting, I must admit, but it wasn't harming me in any way – it was their perverse way of having fun.

I drove around in my car for three weeks with a number plate on the back they had made – with the letters W-A-N-K-E-R. I used to wonder why I would get strange looks at traffic lights! I parked it outside church for three weeks and no one even noticed! At least, they'd not said anything to me.

Then it started getting serious. I found my car tyres slashed a couple of times. I also found that they had tried to sabotage my job in the factory. The boss who owned and ran the factory said I was the only person he could trust to determine what levels of raw materials went into each mixture, because over the years each lad who'd had a grievance against the company had deliberately sabotaged the mixture. He was a Shinto Buddhist, and even though he mocked me for being a Christian he told me that I was the only person he could trust. I then found out that the lads were deliberately not measuring their particular end of the raw materials so that I would probably get sacked. That really did annoy me. Then it got even worse and they started to try to physically harm me.

The overhead crane, for obvious safety reasons, could only be taken up the factory if the hook was well above head height. One day I was working on the floor of the factory, bolting a mould together, with my back to the crane hook which was coming up the factory. The noise of the crane never used to bother me at all because you just got so used to it. I didn't realise that the person who was operating the hook had deliberately lined it up to hit me as it came up the factory. It got me square in the back, knocked the wind out of me completely, and sent me flying. I must say I did everything not to cry – it was such a massive metal hook.

Every night I used to go home and pray, 'Lord just help me get through this next day and help me show these lads what being a Christian is really all about.' I used to have a sense of humour about things. For instance, the toilets were completely full of pornographic magazines – I used to pick all the porn mags out of one toilet, pile them in the other toilet and make a big sign for the door saying 'porn free bog'. I just thought it was a good way of showing my faith without being too prudish. That didn't work because they still ended up coming back into the toilet that I used, and so I then started shredding up their favourite pictures and flushing them away. When they found out I must admit that didn't go down at all well. But I enjoyed it!

It got to the stage where I could take it off most of the lads in the factory but there was one character who wound everybody up. He was the lad who was from Norwich. Nobody particularly liked him; he had a real mean streak in him. He was a bit of a head case and really had it in for me. He always took it that one stage further . . .

Every month the factory would stop production for a morning and we would clean up. This meant cleaning out the moulds, the mixers, the floor and generally making it tidy and safe. My job (because I was small) was to get inside the mixer, which was like an enormous cement mixer and chip all the old mixture off the blades with a pneumatic drill. Obviously this meant turning the power off the mixer to make it completely safe. I remember drilling away one day and just stopping my drill for a minute to get rid of some of the old mix. Even though my ears were ringing from this drill, I heard the very distinctive buzz of the transformer starting on the mixer. This could only mean one thing – that the power had been turned on. I knew I had to get out of that mixer as quickly as possible or I would be killed – the blades would start spinning and that would be the end of me! I had a matter of seconds to get out, so I leapt to my feet, chucked the drill out of the top hatch and climbed up on to one of the blade arms. Just as I pushed out the top hatch, the blade that my leg was on just started to spin round. I just made it out. This nutter from Norfolk had deliberately switched on the power and, whether he meant to or not, could have quite easily killed me. That really did affect me. I could put up with all the messing about, the jokes, and the taunting but that was complete lunacy!

Later that month I'd had a particularly bad week. I'd already turned my car over on the way to work and ended up in a river. One lunchtime we were playing cricket – we'd made this big heavy cricket bat out of some pallet planks. I was batting, the lad from Norfolk was the backstop and somebody else was bowling. This lad had been on at me all day long. I can remember him saying something that was particularly offensive. I can't even remember what it was now – probably something directed at either my mum or my girlfriend. And I just flipped. I turned round with this cricket bat and hit him as hard as I could on the side of his legs. He went down like a felled tree, but I then continued to hit him with the cricket bat. I didn't whack him round the head, but I just kept whacking him. After about the fifth hit – the voice inside my head said, 'What on earth are you doing?' All the lads were shouting 'Go on, kill him!' – they were really loving it, as they didn't particularly like him either. But this voice said, 'You are going to lose your job, you're going to jail and this bloke is going to sue you for damages.' I just stopped and burst out crying. Throwing the bat down I said to him, 'I am really, really, really sorry.' This lad, who was ten inches taller and about four stone heavier than me, just looked at me with frightened eyes and said, 'That's alright, I deserved it.'

Anyway, I got a good talking to by the boss and was told to go home early. I went home and cried my eyes out. I felt I'd completely blown my witness and put them off Jesus for ever. I said sorry to God for all that I'd done.

The next day I went to work very sheepishly, not really anticipating what the lads would do or whether I'd even have a job. But the lads were completely different to me! They didn't even wind me up (they were probably scared that I was going to hit them with a cricket bat!). They had actually seen a human side to me and one by one they approached me and they talked about genuine prayer requests they had. One was in trouble with his marriage, another one's mum was ill with cancer, and another one had a disabled brother. They were asking me to pray for them. It was unbelievable – I really thought I'd blown my witness and yet this was the breakthrough! They had probably seen me as Super-Christian, able to withstand all this pressure and persecution. But as soon as I showed a bit of my human side they warmed to me and they started to respond to my faith. It was a brilliant opportunity. From that point on I was one of the boys and they genuinely respected me, which felt very odd!

Soon after this the YTS boy had his finger chopped off in one of the machines. The Shinto Buddhist manager, who was very superstitious, turned to me and said, 'Andrew, are you an exorcist?' I looked very puzzled and said, 'You what, Mr Kato?' He said, 'You get rid of demons, yes?' I said, 'Well, if anybody asks me to, yes I suppose I do!' He said, 'OK, next Wednesday, we will shut down the whole factory and you will bring your Bible and you will pray and you will get rid of the evil spirit that cut Ken's finger off and tried to kill you. Then we will have a big barbecue with lots of alcohol.' All the lads cheered! I sort of said, 'Well, yes, OK, Mr Kato.'

The following Wednesday the boss got all the workers out of the factory – about 35 in all. They stood in the car park getting the barbecue ready, and I was able to go round the whole factory praying for each individual worker. I didn't cast any evil spirit out of the place or anything like that, but I did pray for each individual. I prayed for safety (it was such a dangerous place with accidents happening all the time). I prayed for a lot more unity and love about the place, as everybody was stabbing each other in the back and sniping about each other. When I had finished praying, I opened the big double doors which led out into the car park feeling like John Wayne coming out of a gun fight! As I went out, people came to me and said, 'Oh did you see anything? Did anything confront you?' I had a chuckle to myself and said, 'Some things are best not talked about.' I really loved it! Then Mr Kato came over and gave me a cheque – I liked getting paid to pray!

It was a fantastic opportunity and from that day until I left six months later there wasn't a single accident in the whole of the factory. The atmosphere in the factory among the workers improved as well. Mr Kato used to stand at the side of the clocking-in machine to say goodbye to everybody and then he would to say to me, 'Ah, Andrew – no accidents this week.' 'Yes Mr Kato – that's God!'

What a fantastic God we have. I thought I'd blown it, but you only need to be open to God, accept his forgiveness when you make mistakes, and just get on with things. God really does help you.

Questions

1. How do you feel when people mock you?
2. How do you hide the 'real you' from other people?
3. Does it make them respect you more when you show your vulnerability?

DEAD

'I don't deny,' he said, 'that there should be priests to remind men that they will one day die. I only say that at certain strange epochs it is necessary to have another kind of priest, called poets, actually to remind men that they are not dead yet . . .' (From G. K. Chesterton's novel, *Manalive*)

Discuss!

20

Walk the Plank!

Baz Gascoyne

Earlier this year I visited a friend who lives and works in Romania. He has been working with street children for over six years now and has seen God provide for this work in many amazing ways. I first had the privilege of visiting the work in 1999 and it was tremendous to go back and see how things had developed and to visit some of the children I had met before. A colleague and I went to see how we could get involved in supporting this work as a church, practically as well as financially. God spoke to me through the different situations and circumstances we came across. I saw more than 20 young people climb out of the hole underground that was their home, as we met a young boy who had been living in one of the homes but longed to go back to living on the streets to beg for his survival. People I met on my first visit who used to live on the streets were now living and working at the farm. God had started to develop their self image, as they felt valued by the love that had been shown them and the opportunity given to them of being able to work and develop new skills.

I met a girl of about 15 living in one of the homes and studying at school. Her face was a picture while she showed me her work and her beautiful neat writing. I felt so excited for her and yet her friend of the same age had decided to stay on the streets and become a prostitute. You cannot help be affected by this, as you see the contrast of their young lives.

I would encourage every man reading this book to go and visit a mission, whether it be in this country or abroad, that is working with people like this. It will do you only good as you see how fortunate you are, but more importantly God will once again break your heart emotionally and spiritually. Your desire will be that of determination to make the most of every opportunity God gives you to serve him faithfully in all that you do.

I left that country, humbled, broken and asking God to forgive me for my often selfish and ungrateful attitude. I wanted to be open to him to use me at any time in any way to bring hope to people. On the journey back to the UK, my mind was running a hundred miles per hour with the images we had seen and the stories we had heard. On our final flight to Manchester from Frankfurt, God challenged and encouraged me as he began to take me at my word. As the plane began to fill up, I said to God, 'If you want me to talk to anyone about you I'm open for that.' I was sitting nearest the aisle, when a gentleman came and asked if he could get to his window seat. No one else came and sat in our section, so we had three seats between the two of us. As the plane began to move down the runway, this man began to grab the side of his face and make some strange noises. At first I wasn't sure if he was afraid of flying, but it became obvious that he was in some distress and pain.

He could not sit still. He kept pressing his handkerchief tightly against his left cheekbone while wincing and constantly moving his head into different positions. Once we were in the air he asked a steward for some painkillers as he had severe toothache. It was then I felt God say to me, 'Why don't you pray for him?'

'Let's just see how the painkillers work shall we?' was my reply.

But he continued to do his armchair dance with sound effects! So, as the stewards came around with drinks he asked them what painkillers they had given him, as they were not working. He was informed that they could only give out asprins. A lady in front of us turned round and asked him if he would like some Nurofen, to which he quickly responded. She told him she would get them out of her bag once the stewards' trolleys were out of the way.

I knew I had to ask him if he would like me to pray for him. It was either Jesus or Nurofen. I had to ask him before the trolleys moved further down the aisle. There was no way Nurofen was going to get the better of Jesus! So I leaned over to this guy and said, 'Excuse me, sir, I'm a minister of a church.' I asked if he would like me to pray for him so that God would heal him. He replied, 'Yes.' So I prayed the following: 'God you know the discomfort Peter is in. Will you please now come and heal him of all the pain so he can enjoy the rest of the flight, in Jesus' name? Amen.' He echoed the Amen quite loudly, and I turned round to see if anyone was looking! He grabbed my hand and thanked me. Minutes later he was taking the tablets. I prayed in my mind and under my breath for about another 20 minutes asking God to do something in this man's life. As the captain informed us of our descent to Manchester, Peter leaned over to me and said the pain had immediately started to go once I prayed for him.

Life in the Spirit

I was introduced to the Holy Spirit about four years after I became a Christian. I now know that he came into my life on the day of my conversion but no one explained that to me. When I was at a Methodist bible college we would have a weekend every so often where a visiting speaker would hold a 'Life in the Spirit' weekend. He or she would speak on the Saturday evening in the chapel to the student body and staff, and again on the Sunday morning.

This particular weekend the speaker spoke about being filled with the Holy Spirit. I sat there listening to this man, wondering who he was talking about, until he explained what Jesus said about the Holy Spirit in John's Gospel chapters 14 and 16. As I sat and listened I felt quite scared and unsure, as I had not heard teaching like this before. At the end of the meeting he offered to pray for anyone who wanted to be baptised or filled with the Holy Spirit. Quite a lot of students responded and went out for prayer. My four friends all went out to be prayed for and I quickly and quietly left the chapel and went to my room. I had many questions racing through my mind as well as fears about what I heard and saw as people were being prayed for. Some of the students began to fall over, others just stood there looking quite peaceful and others started to speak in a different language, which I later found out to be a new prayer language called speaking in tongues.

After the meeting had finished my mates came to my room and started to discuss what had happened to them while they were being prayed for. As I listened to their different experiences I started to feel angry that I had not been told earlier about the Holy Spirit and what he could and would do if we gave permission. My friends had all experienced different things, from a sense of a deep love, identity and peace to a greater awareness of who God was in their lives. Even though I knew I could do with all the above and more, I refused when they offered to pray for me. That night I did not do much sleeping but lots of questioning.

'Was this real or just hype?' 'Was the Holy Spirit really the exact representation of Jesus?' 'If I allowed him into my life fully would it make a difference to my Christian life?' 'Would I have to speak in tongues and sound as if I was saying "She came on a Honda," "Keys for my Sierra", or "Let's have a shandy"?'

The next morning we had our morning service in the chapel. The last thing I wanted was to listen to that bloke again. When he got up to speak, I tried to switch off but couldn't.

He began by explaining he was going to speak on a particular theme but believed God wanted him to speak again on the Holy Spirit. I don't remember anything from what he said; all I do remember is him saying, 'I believe there is one person who needs to come and see me afterwards in the vestry. I would like to pray for them and their fears about the Holy Spirit.' I knew he meant me but how did he know?

I left the chapel as if I was going to my room as most of the students headed for the dining room for lunch. When I thought the coast was clear, I headed for the vestry. I knocked on the door and entered. The gentleman was sitting there. I introduced myself, sat down and he began to ask me some questions. I was only in there for what seemed five minutes when he asked if he could pray for me. I didn't feel anything but was impressed with what he prayed. It was something like the following: 'God, you know this young man wants to serve and follow you the rest of his life. He knows he can't do this in his own strength and needs you to help him. Will you come now by your Spirit and fill him to overflowing with your love and peace? Take away all the fears he has of what might happen or what he should feel, and surprise him with the difference you will make in his life. Amen.'

I thanked him and went for my lunch, trusting God to answer his prayer. As I went on studying at college I was aware of how God was changing me and helping me. His prayers were being answered.

Months later after leaving college I was working for a friend of mine from church. Alan was a farmer and needed some help to do some potato-picking. I needed the money as I was unemployed and I didn't mind doing it. The work consisted of me and two other fellows standing at the back of a trailer being pulled by the tractor. As the spuds were being dug up they would come up a conveyor belt to where we stood. Our job was to sort the spuds from the soil so they could then go up another conveyor belt and be stored in the trailer being pulled alongside us. Eight hours a day of this and you soon get bored.

After a few days I decided to take my personal stereo headset so I could listen to the radio or tapes to kill the boredom. One day I was listening and singing to a tape of a Christian band when out of the blue this strange language started to come out of my mouth. The two guys I was working with began to look at me as if I had just landed from another planet. I certainly was singing as if I had!

What in the world was going on? One minute everything was fine; the next all chaos had broken out. I remember coming up with some explanation for the guys, which they bought. However, every time I went to speak there was this urge to speak in this different language. I could not wait for the day to finish so I could see my mate and ask him what was going on.

When I got to his house and he opened the door I asked him, 'What's this?' I opened my mouth and out it came. My mate smiled and said, 'That's tongues.'

'Why would God give it to me on the back of a tractor,' I asked? 'I thought it only happened when someone prayed for you at the end of a meeting.'

'God has given you this gift, so use it and don't abuse it. It is there to help you pray and worship, so just do that.'

This was the beginning of an awareness of who and what the Holy Spirit's role is in the Christian life.

In 1995 at the City Hall in Sheffield, a big cuddly man from California came over to Britain with a team to do numerous conferences around the country. His name was John Wimber, and it seemed people either loved him or hated him. I had never heard of this man but I went to the conference which was all about Jesus using you by the leading of the Holy Spirit. It was tremendous to be in a packed hall with people worshipping God and to see the hunger there was from the delegates to hear about being more effective in sharing their faith.

During the first session John told his story of how God came into his life and dramatically change his lifestyle. At the end of his talk he encouraged us all to stand and said, 'God is here by his Spirit and wants to come and minister to each person in whatever way he chooses for you, to help you be more effective in the calling that's on your life.'

As we stood Wimber spoke those famous words which were to annoy many and bless thousands, 'Come Holy Spirit.'

I was wondering if I was caught up in some clip from the film *The Blues Brothers*!

After a short while some people began to cry, shake, laugh or fall over, while others like me just stood staring at the things that were happening to them. I must admit I was feeling apprehensive and wondering if I was caught up in some clip from the film *The Blues Brothers*! Others stood silently with their eyes closed looking quite peaceful.

Wimber encouraged his team to begin moving among the people and start praying for them. One of the Americans came up to me and said he believed that God had spoken to him about a situation in my life. He continued to say that God had shown him that when I was 15 I was sexually interfered with. I could not believe what I was hearing! He was spot on, but I was not going to admit he was right as I was embarrassed and angry with God that he would reveal such a thing. So as casually as possible, and without blushing, I said to this guy, 'I'm sorry but you're wrong.' He graciously apologised and moved on to pray for others. When I got home that night I sat for a while wondering how God had shown this man what had happened to me and why? The next day I was back at the conference hoping to hear from God, longing to be encouraged but also open to be challenged by him about areas of my life where sin ruled. When people were given the opportunity to receive prayer at the end of the meeting, I stood.

Then I noticed the guy from the previous night approaching me. 'Please God don't do this to me,' I thought. He smiled and immediately apologised as he began to say the following: 'Last night I could not sleep as I believe God was speaking to me about you and what I shared with you last night. He told me that I had not made a mistake and told me not to embarrass you but to heal you, so you no longer would be emotionally tied to that incident in your life.' I looked at him with two thoughts running through my head, if that is possible for a man! They were 'Will you please sod off?' and the other was 'Please let this be true'.

I stood there looking at him in silence, which seemed ages. Eventually I said to him, 'You are right – I'm sorry for lying to you yesterday.' He just smiled and encouraged me to talk to a friend I could trust and let God begin the healing process.

How amazing God is. He sends over a guy from America who has never even been to this country before, never mind not knowing me, but allows God to speak to him in such a way that God breaks into an area of my life that I had been carrying around for over ten years. I will always be grateful to God and to that guy for his holy obedience and for stepping out in faith.

That night I chose to tell my best mate Steve. As I sat in his lounge with his wife Janice I told him what had happened in the meeting. With a lot of fear I told them what had happened to me when I was 15 while I was having a trial for a football team. As I shared about the player coach sexually interfering with me, I waited for the look of disgust and the barrage of words coming back at me saying how they did not want our friendship to continue. How wrong I was! Steve came over to me and hugged me, and slowly I began to cry until I could not control my emotions. I wept uncontrollably with tears streaming down my face, and snot running down my nose on to my mate's shirt, but he just kept hugging me. This was the beginning of God healing me of all the hurt, anger, hatred and pain that I had bottled up.

During the next few days at the conference I began to discover and experience more of God's love and power, as I heard stories of ordinary men and women being guided by the Holy Spirit to share their faith with people, pray for healing and even share words of knowledge and prophecy to people inside the church as well as outside. I remember saying to God in the final meeting of that conference, 'God, whatever you want to do in my life, do it, and I will try and be open and obedient to you so you can.'

Whenever anyone prays a prayer like that I imagine God rubbing his hands together and saying to Jesus, the Holy Spirit and the angels, 'Now we are going to have some fun.'

It was not long after this that I began to experience God speaking to me in ways that had not happened before. Yes, he was still speaking to me through the Bible, when I prayed and when I went to church, but now he was speaking to me through pictures in my mind, thoughts and even pains in different parts of my body or heat in my hands. Sometimes I would be walking through the city centre and I would look at someone and then get a thought in my mind. It could be depression, hurt, sorrow or anger. I wish I could say that I always responded to these promptings from God, but I didn't.

Two occasions when I did step out created quite a stir. The first situation was on a Sunday morning. I had been asked the day before if I would play for a football team as their goalkeeper was away: I was happy to oblige. The morning of the match I woke up with quite a sharp pain in my back. I didn't know what was wrong, but it was sore. I played football that morning rather badly due to this constant pain.

After lunch I laid down on the settee as the pain increased. I was supposed to be speaking at a Methodist church in the evening. Eventually the pain was so severe that I decided to phone the church to explain that I would not be able to make the meeting that evening. As I struggled to get to the phone, I felt as if the Holy Spirit was whispering to me, 'Don't cancel – go.' I started to argue with God, 'Why should I go when I'm in so much pain?' He replied, 'Because the pain you are in is what one of the members of the church has been suffering for years. Tonight I want to heal them.' As I got ready for the service, I asked God what was wrong with the person. He replied they had had a trapped nerve in the spine.

I managed to drive to the church building and meet the people before the service started. As we began the service, the pain was getting more and more unbearable. I was pleased to get to the point where I was to speak. There were about 50 people in the church. I explained what had happened to me and what I believed God had said about someone having that pain for years but tonight he wanted to heal them. Straightaway, this lady called Joan stood up and said, 'I'm healed. The pain has gone.' She started jumping and dancing around while we all looked on in amazement. I also thought, 'Great! I carry this pain around all day and don't even get the opportunity to pray with her! I wonder why?'

The lady next to Joan saw what God had done and that night knew God was real. Within a week the whole street where Joan lived knew about her healing, including her husband, who responded, 'I know this is real because something has happened to you.'

I spoke to Joan while writing this chapter to make sure I had the facts right. Joan had been in constant pain for over five years with sciatica and God began his healing in her life that night. What really surprised me when talking to Joan was that the pain did not fully leave her until Wednesday, and I still had the pain when I left the church, right up to Wednesday!

I wanted to be used more like this for God, so people's lives could be changed, whether they were Christians or not, and for Jesus to become more real in people's lives.

The second occasion when I got a severe pain did not cause such a joyous reaction. I worked at the YMCA and organised a monthly meeting called 'Powerpoint' for teenagers from different churches in and around the city. The evening consisted of a Christian artist or band, plus a speaker who would challenge and encourage the teenagers to commit their lives to God and follow him. The evenings would attract anything from 200 to 600 teenagers, both Christians and those who didn't know Jesus yet.

One particular evening, my mate Steve was speaking and we had a group from York called Mimic, which included a mime artist and a soloist who played the guitar and keyboards. I remember the evening was a fancy dress night.

During the day I started to get a severe pain in my left testicle, again very painful while trying to play football. By the evening the pain had worsened and I was wondering if this was about someone who was going to be at the meeting. I shared this with Steve and his response was 'Well, I'm not sharing that – you can!' I said to him, 'Let's pray that if this is God wanting to heal someone then the pain will get worse.'

Afterwards I wasn't sure that was such a clever prayer! The evening began. Most people had arrived in fancy dress as it was the Christmas special. The mime artists were excellent. Steve spoke well, and then we got to the response. By this time I was in serious discomfort. Steve had asked people to respond to whatever God had been saying to them. People became Christians, others were doing business with God about some area in their lives and others asked for prayer for healing in their lives. God was moving in that place and it was quite amusing to see people in fancy dress being prayed for.

Steve then came over to me and asked how the pain was. When I replied 'worse' he looked at me as if to say 'Great'! He then went back to the microphone and said, 'Baz would like to say something.' My heart was pounding, my testicle aching, and I thought, 'Please God, let this be you, and not me drawing attention to myself.' I wasn't sure how you talk about a left testicle in a Christian meeting. If it was a group of guys playing football and someone had the ball kicked in that region we would know what to say, but I didn't want to offend anyone!

Well, eventually I began to speak and said, 'I believe tonight that God wants to heal a guy (it certainly wasn't going to be a girl, Baz!) who has a problem with their left testicle.' As sensitively as possible I encouraged this person to talk to a close friend after the meeting or in the next few days and get them to pray for their healing. I certainly was not going to ask them to come to the front for prayer and be embarrassed in front of the rest of the young people.

I was pleased I had shared what I believed God wanted me to, but nothing had prepared me for what happened next. A whole group of people got up and walked out of the building, obviously not happy with what I had shared. This caused me a lot of anxiety, as I knew these people and did not want to upset them or anyone else. People continued to pray for one another. When everyone had gone and just a few of us were left to tidy up, I asked Steve to pray for me as I was feeling very vulnerable that I had caused others to be upset.

Later, when all the equipment was cleared away, I was in my office collecting a few things before I left for home. There was a knock on my door and a guy called James (not his real name) who worked at the YMCA asked if he could have a chat. He eventually informed me that he was the person with the left testicle problem. It was twisted and he had a cyst on it and was due to go to the hospital on Monday to have it looked at. I asked him if he would like me to pray for him, which he agreed. I asked God to finish what he had started and heal James of this problem. He left and I thanked God for encouraging me.

First thing on Monday morning I had an assembly to do and then I went to the YMCA. Later on that morning James came to see me to tell me how he had got on at the hospital. The cyst had gone and his testicle had gone back to the correct position – God had healed him!

I tell you these stories not to blow my own trumpet but

hopefully to encourage you to step out for God when he speaks to you. The most important thing to remember is that God will not speak to you about a situation or person and ask you to do something about it and leave you by yourself. He will be with you. The Christian life is exciting and challenging, so why not let God take you on this adventure as he carries you along by his Spirit?

Questions

1. What was your first experience of the Holy Spirit?
2. What has been your most memorable experience of the Holy Spirit? Where was this? Why was this?
3. When was the last time you gave yourself totally to the Holy Spirit? How did you feel? Did anything happen?
4. In the book of Ezekiel chapter 47:1–12, we read about the river from the temple. How would you grade yourself today in connection with the picture that Ezekiel describes about the Holy Spirit?
   Are you
   - ankle deep
   - knee deep
   - waist deep
   - submerged, swimming with your feet not being able to touch the bottom?
5. Have you any fears of the Holy Spirit?
6. Have you had a bad experience in the past which is holding you back?
7. Why do we need the Holy Spirit?
8. Since the Holy Spirit is dwelling in the believer, isn't that enough?

OVERFLOWING

'I must be filled. It is absolutely necessary.
I may be filled. God has made it blessedly possible.
I want to be filled. It is eminently desirable.
I will be filled. It is so blessedly certain.'

(Andrew Murray, quoted in *What Great Evangelicals Believed about the Holy Spirit 1850–1930* by Leona Frances Choy, Christian Publications, Pennsylvania, 1990)

21

What Women *Really* Want

EMMA FLINT

'A woman needs a man like a fish needs a bicycle.' (Irina Dunn)

My degree was sociology – which one of my mates tells me is the study of things that don't need to be studied by the people who do! I disagree! The most fun I had was the course I did on society and sexuality. My seminar group consisted of me, five lesbians and one straight bloke (who lasted two sessions). Our topics for discussions included 'the deconstruction of the male penis' and 'a world without men, is it possible?'.

Now, I thought I was a feminist but this group informed me that I was nowhere near! They really didn't enjoy the fact that I was a Christian, and when I got engaged halfway through the course, they hung their heads in sheer disappointment.

I liked the phrases 'post-feminism' and 'gender reconciliation' and would always throw them into our discussions. The others saw them as complete compromise, but I see them as kingdom values of working together and living as God intended.

You men should not have to carry the burden of centuries of patriarchy. We can work from where we are now by changing people's attitudes by the way that we live. I reckon actions and words speak about as loud as each other.

I have struggled over this whole man and woman thing, as the Bible seems to contain contradictions and people make it say whatever they want to say. But we can't get away from the fact that we are all made in God's image. And then there is Jesus . . . I had a hard job at uni trying to explain that Jesus treated women with radical respect. I reckon this is not because they misunderstood Jesus, but because the church has not really demonstrated this Christ-like attitude.

> I think Jesus was a feminist. Actually, I think he was an unbelievably revolutionary, gutsy feminist, considering the status of women in his time . . . He just constantly upended the patriarchal assumptions of his day. But I believe, as many Christians do, that there is a huge chasm between what Jesus said and what the church has created. (Naomi Wolf, *Third Way* journal, December 2001. Vol 24. No 9. – p.23)

Some people, some of the time

I hate generalisations, especially those about men and women. Some of the ones I heard this week include: 'All girls say the opposite of what they really mean'; 'Girls take longer than men to get ready'; 'Girls can't read maps'; 'Men can't wrap presents'; 'Girls can't throw over-arm'; 'Blokes don't show their emotions'; 'Real men have scars'; 'Men should put out the rubbish' (well, that one might have a point . . . !).

It really bugs me when things like shopping, Earl Grey tea, salt-and-vinegar crisps, the colour pink, *The Sound of Music*, or crying, are described as 'a girl thing' when actually men need to realise that it is OK to like these things too! What bugs me even more is when lads are called 'you big girl' as a put-down. It's often used when a bloke has actually expressed how he feels or said something sensitive.

We should label jars not people

The church has done a great job at reinforcing the traditional gender stereotypes, and in doing so it has missed out on so much over the years. I love the film *Shrek* because it illustrates how we should not judge a book by its cover. We should label jars not people and not assume one person is the same as another.

We're not lovin it, lovin it, lovin it . . .

Let's get this one thing clear. No girl I know enjoys being referred to as 'bird'. Some things just aren't funny. Can we think about what we call each other?

As for 'the time of the month', I feel sorry for you guys because there really doesn't seem to be a good way to handle it. Whatever you do or say seems to be wrong. We are sorry. It isn't much fun for us, but we should try not to take it out on you and use it as a total excuse for mouthing off. I guess my advice is: chocolate does help, whatever the doctors say! Before we were married, my husband (a doctor) once sent me a Ryvita in the post at the difficult time (because apparently that's what we really need). I have never seen a Ryvita since. It just didn't help!

Maybe I am 'hypersensitive' as some men like to call me, but I think there are certain things that aren't funny. Don't get me wrong, I am a good laugh and can take a joke. (I have to put up with enough stick as a Man United fan in Leeds.) But we need to honour one another with what we say and guard our speech.

As men and women of God, we need to be better at speaking out the positive to each other. As a woman in church leadership and working for a Christian charity, I need a lot of encouragement. I do get it from my husband and girlfriends, but in general I don't get many compliments about my work from the blokes around me. Blokes that I know well will tend to say, 'You know what I think about you, don't you?' when actually they haven't ever really told me.

I am not asking for them to tell me I look good (well that would be nice!), just give some positive encouragement now and then. We need to be secure in our relationships with each other so that we can give compliments and receive them too. We need to be sure where we stand with each other. We ladies have a responsibility to speak affirming words to our men. And to speak in an honouring way about them.

One thing that I really want to know: what do men talk about on their lads' nights out? I know that we want men to talk about us when they go out with their mates, but I just don't think that it happens! Girls talk about men all the time! Get this, I was just at a girl sleep-over the other night. A group of us went through all the men in our church and said what it is we like about them (without mentioning any body parts!). We really appreciated our amazing male friends. Could men do that about the ladies?

Together for ever . . .

Men need to release women and show us that we are needed. It is not a competition but all about reconciliation and affirming what gifts and wisdom are there in us all. We don't want to be like men, but we do want the same opportunities to be ourselves and speak, worship and prophesy in our own way. It does after all seem that the fellas still get the most important jobs and decisions to make. I guess we just want the boys to understand that many women are having to operate in what still seems like a man's world.

We are the image of God together. There is still a lack of female leaders and role models in the church. A friend of mine came to a leaders' lunch the other day and was shocked at the low turnout of women there. I had been particularly pleased that week because there were five! It is sometimes difficult to speak when you are in such a minority. It seems that you get heard better if your voice has broken!

The church has a huge responsibility to mirror the image of God; to live out and demonstrate what it is to be fully human. The fact is that we do annoy each other and wind each other up (a lot). Then it's down to how we deal with that. We should be slow to anger and quick to make up.

'Hello! I am just having an opinion'

I hate the fact that I am always called PC for bringing people into line for out-of-order comments, or called 'feisty' for having an opinion. Feisty is what my granddad called the horse that was the most hassle. We want to be passionate and 'have spirit' but most of all to be full of God and grace and be listened to.

My husband and his male friends shocked me at first because they didn't put each other down. Instead they would hug and sit on each other's knee. (I think the next-door neighbour was very surprised when Rob announced his engagement to me.) But it was liberating to meet men that would say how they felt to each other and even compliment each other.

My girlfriends and I made a list of all that we want out of men. Here is the reduced version, so that men will read it!

Gentle. Cries. Funny. Sensitive. Manly. Muscley. Cooks (like Jamie Oliver). Romantic. Respected. Passionate. God is the most important thing to him. Relational. Has good CD collection. Likes children. Radical. Speaks his mind. Brings out the best in me. Prays a lot. Really close to God. Real. Not a wimp. Drinks Earl Grey! Empowering. Encouraging. Sexy. Someone our mum and sister will like. Doesn't have sweaty pits. Good body. Takes care of their appearance. Can have girly chats. Has nice underpants. Secure. Not dominating. Exciting. Adventurous. Surprises us. No greasy hair. No bad breath!

No pressure then lads! (ed).

Many of my girlfriends struggle with the fact that so many Christian men are too 'christiany', if you know what I mean. Sensitive doesn't have to mean wussy! But at the end of the day all we really want are men who love God, love people, and are free to be themselves. We want the best brought out of us, so please can we have less focus on what we look like and more releasing of who we are in God?

The thing that will get people's attention is the way we love one another. We need to get over the problems that surround us in society and live out lives that reflect the freedom we have, being secure in our identities. The church needs, in the words of Billy Bragg, 'man and woman together'. Let's keep working on it.

Questions

1. Has anything in this chapter challenged you about your language towards women?
2. Why are there still so few women in Christian leadership?
3. Can you handle being beaten by a woman – at sport, for instance?

NO MORE MEN?

Now that your wife can earn a lot more than you (mine does), what's the point of a man? Wouldn't the world be a better place if we were killed at birth and our seed preserved for the continuation of the race? Just think – no more wars – nations would just gossip and bitch about each other. Sounds good, doesn't it? And the women don't really help. They want you to be hard on the outside, but soft on the inside; commanding, but liberated, strong but not domineering, a master lover who never looks at another woman . . . and earning loads of money would help too.

With women now coming into their own we need a new understanding of masculinity. If we're no longer holding the strings of power as the providers of food and shelter, we need to be seeking God for new understandings of how to honour him through who we are. I think men and women *are* different, but the fact that women are slowly showing themselves to be just as good as us in the workplace has helped make sense of the rather worldly hard-working wife of Proverbs 31.

(Simon)

22
Zany Gob Case
BAZ GASCOYNE

Have you ever been encouraged by your friends to do something which you later regretted? This was always happening to me when I was a teenager, and unfortunately I would never back down. We would dare each other regularly, hoping that someone would fail or be caught. A dare back home was called a 'duffer'. Interestingly one of the meanings of this word is 'something worthless or useless', but to us it was everything.

I remember vividly two duffers that were given to me which had a huge impact on my life. Both were when I was about 15 years old. The first was when about six of us were round a girl's house, trying to impress her and her mates. We had all been drinking our token can of lager or bottle of cider between the six of us. So when we were leaving the house one of my friends shouted, 'Follow the leader.' This was a command for the rest of us to do whatever he decided to do. It could be banging on someone's door, window or something else. As he ran away from the house with the girls looking on, he decided to jump over a car. Not just any car but a bright yellow Lotus Elite. So he jumped on the bonnet and ran over the top, leaping off the back end, closely followed by the rest of us. Two, three, four, five were all over cleanly, waiting and watching for me, but my foot slipped and landed on the windscreen. There was a huge crack, which appeared just as someone looked from behind the curtains and saw us all standing around the car and me still on it. We all ran down the street and split up in various directions as the owner of the car began driving down the street after us. We were never caught, but our underpants needed to be changed swiftly when we all arrived at our homes.

The second occasion was when I was going out with a girl named Charlotte (not her real name) who I was really fond of. We had been going out with each other for over a year. Every Tuesday evening, my mates and I would go to Mowden Park Rugby Club disco, which was specially put on for under 18s. We used to have a great time dancing, watching others, having a laugh and snogging. This particular evening a group of us were walking home when I was asked by one of my mates if I had fondled Charlotte's breasts yet. My silence and embarrassment answered his question, which he then started to tease me about. He 'duffered' me to do so. As we walked home we had to cross a field where Charlotte and I started to kiss, and before she could do anything I put my hand up her blouse and touched one of her breasts. Immediately, she pulled away and began crying and ran off home. I ran after her to apologise but she told me to get lost. I felt such a prat. I had given in once again to peer pressure and ended up regretting it, but more importantly hurting someone I cared for.

The reason for these stories is to illustrate how easily we

are affected by what others think of us, and why we often do what they want in order to be accepted by them. This attitude easily flows into the church and affects how we behave as Christians. A friend of mine was encouraged to become a local preacher in the Methodist church many years ago. Every time he got into the pulpit to preach he would faint. This happened about three times and every time he would come round with a bunch of ladies splashing water over his face and giving him a drink. I remember asking him whether God might be trying to say something to him. He realised later that he should not be preaching.

Shortly after I became a Christian, I felt that there was a calling on my life to communicate the good news of Jesus. However, it seemed that I didn't fit the mould. I now realise that God wants us to be ourselves and allow him to make us what we should be and not what the church wants or thinks we should be.

I have always wanted to be open to bring God's message in whatever way he chooses. Unfortunately I have made mistakes in the past and no doubt will in the future, but hope I will be humble enough to admit this and repent where needed and apologise when required. When you get to this point in your Christian life, you put yourself in a position of being misunderstood or written off by other Christians. This is why it is important to be accountable to people and have true friends who will love, protect and correct you.

In the last eight years or so I think I have started to discover how some of the biblical characters must have felt, especially the prophets, due to some of their bizarre behaviour in bringing God's message. In 1995 an American couple came to Sheffield and prophesied over my wife and me. Part of the word was, 'And though your actions seem bizarre now, some in the future will seem even more bizarre because there is a proclamation of prophecy that needs to be seen.' As this was spoken over us, I got very excited and shouted and jumped up and down. This was not because I felt important or special. It was because I felt God was encouraging me by saying, 'It's OK, you are on the right track; you have not lost your marbles.'

When I began to carry a stick around with me, either to worship God or pray with, this always caused a stir among the Christians. I went to a citywide prayer event, where there must have been up to 300 people. I had been in the meeting about five minutes when a leader came up to me and asked if I would put the stick down. So I politely asked why. His response was 'Because we do not have a theology for sticks!' Isn't it funny how as soon as we (myself included) don't understand something of what God is doing, we try to theologise it rather than talking to the people concerned? If you were to come to my house, you would see I have a basket-load of sticks all sizes and shapes, in my dining room, which represent different things to help me when I pray. I have a stick I use which represents healing, and another with people's names on so I can hold it and pray for the people on the stick. I was given a stick from a friend in Leeds, so when I use that I pray for the city of Leeds. For a long time I would stand or dance around a Union Jack banging my stick in the middle of the flag. It was a few months after I had been doing this before I felt God gave me understanding of what was happening. He told me that for every time I hit the flag with the stick, it would represent another person entering the kingdom of God. As you can imagine I began to bang louder and more frequently. Sometimes I felt I should press the end of the stick gently into the stomach of the person I had been asked to pray for, as God was saying he wanted to do a deep work within that person.

While in America on vacation, I was given a stick at a friend's church barbecue. In their Sunday meeting the next day during the worship our friend Bob felt God was saying that he should play a song on the drums and sing. Bob is part of the worship team of the church and we were to find out later that he has never done this before or since. He told the church he was going to sing 'Kum ba ya my Lord' and Linda and I looked at each other as if to ask 'Did I really hear him right?' What made it more embarrassing was what he said next. He told the church that while he was singing and playing, Baz was going to come out and dance with his stick in front of everyone, as God was going to do something significant for the church that morning. I could not believe what I was hearing! I was going to have to dance to a song I've mocked so many times. How could I dance to that song in a manly way? As Bob encouraged me in the front of the church, all I could say to God was, 'Please help me.'

I stood facing the church, nervously waiting for Bob to start and wondering what these lovely people were thinking. As Bob began to play, I was surprised and rejoicing that the rhythm he was playing was not that of our Sunday school tune but something like an African tribal dance. As he began to sing in a slow and deliberate way I felt the Holy Spirit anoint me and I began to dance. I have been using sticks to worship God for a number of years now as this helps me to do so in a masculine way. This Sunday was no exception; I felt free to be a warrior dancing to and for my God.

What was to happen next surprised Bob, the leaders and me. A few people began to run to the front of the church.

They were crying, kneeling, lying down, and the noise was staggering as people began to pray out loud, 'God, come by here – Please don't pass us by.' People did business with God that morning.

One gentleman named George asked if he could use my stick. As I gave it to him, he shouted out, 'Men, get hold of this stick, as it represents authority.' As the men came and touched the stick, George prayed for them.

Ultimately, it is the Holy Spirit who helps us in our prayers (as we read in Romans 8:26). I brought a stick (similar to a Moses-type staff) back last week from Romania to assist me in my prayers for a friend and the work he is doing among street children. I find it helps me to focus more easily on what I'm praying for as I hold the stick or worship. Standing on a hillside overlooking Sheffield, I feel I can pray and intercede for the city far more passionately with a stick in my hand than without. This does not mean my prayers are more effective than anyone else's – it just means this is right for me and helpful.

When I first began taking sticks into church meetings people were wary, sceptical and cynical. One lady from the church I attended wrote to me saying how she initially related it to that of Indian rain dances and totem poles and did not feel it had much to do with God. However, after talking to one of her friends, her opinion changed. Her friend had informed her that when I banged the stick by them they felt a real outpouring of the Holy Spirit. She went on to say she realised God was saying I needed to bring the sticks into the church as a prophetic statement of what God was doing and is to do in the nation.

In the same year I went to hear two Baptist ministers associated with Toronto Airport Fellowship in Canada.

They shared about their spiritual journey and what God had done in their lives and where he was taking them.

What was to follow was to shock and encourage me at the same time.

During the meeting I had the weird thought that I should pull the heads off the flower display at the front of the church and throw the petals over these two men. I told my friend what I thought and he just smiled at me. Later on there was an opportunity for us to ask these guys any questions about what they had been talking about or anything to do with what God was doing in these days. Many questions were being asked and I thought I would ask them the following: 'Have you come across people in your travels who are doing some strange things in the whole area of prophecy, such as symbolism and acting out things to bring God's message to individuals or churches?' The reason for asking this was that once again I was feeling vulnerable about what God was doing with me and asking of me. Their response was affirmative. But what was to follow was to shock and encourage me at the same time. Rick (one of the guys) replied, 'God has told you to say and do something over us, hasn't he?' 'Yes,' I replied. 'Well, you had better do it at the end of the meeting.' My friend just looked at me and laughed!

At the close of the meeting I went up to both of these men and stood them alongside the large flower display. I had spoken to the leader of this church beforehand, explaining what I felt I should do. Feeling very apprehensive, I began to pull the heads off the flowers until most of them were in my hands. I said to these men that God wanted them to know what it meant to be the fragrance of death to some and the fragrance of life to others, which we read about in 2 Corinthians 2:14–15. I then began to drop these petals on their heads. Before one touched them they were both lying on the floor under the power of God. All I could think of was the mess I was making on the floor, so I kept on saying, 'I'm sorry, I will hoover up after!'

People were still in the church and the looks were varied. Eventually, these two ministers got up and came to talk to me and thanked me for being obedient to God. That morning as they were praying about their time in the UK, they informed me that they actually smelt a sweet fragrance enter the room they were praying in. Their first thought was that it must be the cleaner or the lady of the home. They soon discovered that no one else was in the house but them. God was speaking to them and he confirmed it by the flower petals. God is great.

Some time later Linda and I were praying with some of our friends at their home. I felt I should pour over the husband a large bowl of potpourri that was on their fireplace. I shared this with Linda to see what she thought. My friend heard me talking and said, 'Whatever God is saying, just do it.' So I picked up the bowl and began to pour this over him. As the pieces hit him, God impacted his life in a very powerful way through the Holy Spirit.

A few years later I felt God speak to me about dyeing my hair blonde and having the word FIRE shaved in the back and dyed red. This was to represent that I was praying for God's love to spread through this nation like a forest fire. I was amazed at the reaction I got from people. One of my neighbours called me over and said, 'What the bloody hell is that on the back of your head?' When I told her, she replied, 'We could do with a bit of that in this country.'

I only ever had one negative reaction from a non-Christian and that was when I was with some friends at a bingo hall. After being asked to explain the haircut, some of the staff reacted quite aggressively and told me that they wanted none of that stuff here. Apart from that incident it's interesting that most of the complaints came from Christians.

Later on I kept getting this impression I should shave my head bald and just leave the word on the back. I spoke to my wife Linda about this and asked my friends what they thought, as I didn't particularly want to draw attention to myself. Linda suggested I should wait a while and see what God was trying to say through this.

A few weeks later Linda and I were at a conference, which was for churches who were part of the network we belong to. During one of the meetings a guy got up at the front of the meeting and began to prophesy. He is well respected and trusted among our churches and recognised as a prophet. He began by saying he believed there was going to be a move among men in the whole area of humility. As a sign of this some men had already been challenged by God to shave their heads. I turned to Linda and we just smiled.

It must be difficult at times for my wife to be married to someone like me. Before I shaved my head, I decided to phone the schools that I visit on a regular basis to inform them what I was planning on doing. I didn't want them to think I was encouraging any of the pupils to do likewise. The response I got from the schools was very interesting: none of the schools asked me not to come in while my head was bald. In the staff room of one school a staff member made the following comment: 'At last God is doing something in the church.' People are looking for spiritual guidance and yet we as Christians can often be the stumbling block for them, either by the way we behave or by the way we restrict God from working through us!

I wish I could say to you that every time God has asked me to do something for him I have responded positively and been obedient. It's not that God is asking me to do some strange and wacky things every week. All I'm trying to do is to be open to him when he does speak and try and be faithful to him.

About three years ago I clearly felt God guiding me to begin to wear chains. One of the places was to be at the National Evangelists' Conference held at Swanwick every year. I felt that God wanted to remind the evangelists who attended that they were called by God to preach the good news and break the chains over people's lives through

Please try to imagine me in Homebase, wrapping chains around myself as people passed the aisle.

Jesus, and allow God to break any chains over their own lives that were restricting them from knowing the fullness of life in Christ. After checking this out with the committee who plan the conference, I went to buy the chains. Please try to imagine me in Homebase, wrapping chains around myself as people passed the aisle. They were all looking at me as if I had just escaped from the film set of *One Flew Over the Cuckoo's Nest*. Once I had got enough chains I got one of their assistants to cut them. I felt that each delegate should be offered the chance as part of their response to God to take home with them a chain link to remind them of their calling, so I bought enough to have 350 links. One of the committee members kindly paid for the links.

What was so good about this conference was right at the beginning one of the committee members told the delegates why I was wearing the chains and said they believed it was a prophetic statement to the conference. The speaker for the conference, Jeff Lucas, also referred to the chains during one of his sessions, which again was such a blessing.

I have to admit I still felt vulnerable wearing the chains all day, especially at meal times and when we went out for a curry. However, the way the conference delegates responded was fantastic. Not everyone took a link or fully embraced what I was doing, but I didn't get one negative comment to my face. Behind my back, I'm not so sure! Probably because evangelists are used to flack themselves they were being sensitive to me.

During the next three to four months I wore the chains every Sunday morning at my home church. I was not sure why, but I knew I had to. One Sunday morning a friend of mine (Gary from Bournemouth) was speaking. During his talk he mentioned the prisoners in America who are on death row. When they are about to go to be executed, a guard walks in front of them shouting 'dead man walking' as they follow slowly behind in chains. As soon as I heard this, God said, 'That's why you are wearing these chains – to remind you and the church that there are dead men walking everywhere and *you* are the people to bring them back to life and free them through Jesus.'

The reason this chapter is called 'Zany Gob Case' is because it is an anagram of my name. A friend in my church discovered this a few weeks ago; however, I believe it is God just encouraging and reminding me that I am a fool for Christ and prepared to look a fool in other's eyes to speak out the truth for Jesus. It is not always easy living this way, but it is nothing to the humiliation and pain that Christ went through for you and me.

Are you willing to stand up and be counted for Jesus, whatever he asks of you? Are you willing to be a 'sign and a wonder'?

Questions

1. In what ways did God ask the Old Testament prophets to communicate his message?
2. How would you feel if you were in their shoes (or sandals)?
3. Has God ever asked you to do something you have felt was rather odd? Did you do it?
4. Have you got close friends around you to sound things out with?
5. Are you accountable to anyone? If not, why not?
6. Do you allow yourself to be open to the Holy Spirit to be used in new and creative ways?
7. Read the Gospels again and see how Jesus communicated to different people. What can you learn from this?

Who Is Lee Jackson Anyway?

I was born in 1970 in Billingham in the north-east of England where I lived until I was twelve years old. Then my dad, who had a great job with a company car and all the rest of it, suddenly dropped the bombshell that he was going to become a vicar! So my mum, dad and I moved to St John's College in Nottingham while my dad trained to go into the Anglican ministry. (My sister, Angela, who is seven years older than me, had already been married and had moved away.)

We lived in Nottingham for two-and-a-half years, and I went to Chilwell Comprehensive School and did a lot of BMXing in that time. Then my dad had his first curacy and we all moved to Clifton in York where I went to Cannon Lee School for a year and then onto York sixth form college. I had lost the will to study by the time I got to sixth form and spent most of my time enjoying the parties, and fighting to stay in college while doing as little work as possible! We moved away and I tried to revise for my A-levels, just missing out on getting Sociology – I got an N which means 'nearly', which I think is always a bit of a downer!

I got a job in a solicitor's in the motor accident claims department and I moved on to work in the Civil Service in the Crown Court and the County Court. It was an OK 9 to 5 job and pretty boring at times for me, but at that time I was also doing youth work at St Barnabas Church in Leeds and I had formed the band HOG (or House of God as it was originally called) with Nick Mawby and Justin Thomas. We were the first ever British Christian rap (Hip-Hop) group. We travelled doing festivals and even went abroad once or twice. We connected with the World Wide Message Tribe in Manchester and were their support act for a couple of years, and I still DJ with them now. So when rock and folk were big in the early nineties, we were the only Christian rap group, which always made it interesting for us. We nearly finished our musical careers when we were the support band for a heavy metal band and the audience hated us so much that they started throwing coins at us on the stage.

Then in 1993 I decided to leave my job in the courts to do a YWAM discipleship training course in sunny St Helens in Merseyside. This was an urban ministry course which I did for five months before moving to Northern Ireland in a staunch loyalist environment. Working there was a real eye-opener for me and I learnt such a lot including meeting reformed terrorists and amazing Catholic priests who showed me how Jesus used to live, which changed my view on Catholics for ever.

While away at YWAM I had a telephone call from Doreen McConnell. She had been praying for a schools worker for several years, as even a city the size of Leeds with three quarters of a million people had no Christian schools work to speak of and we really wanted to set something up fast. So she asked me if I'd like a job that didn't exist, and I said 'That sounds great – what *is* a schools worker?' I started work on 1st September 1994 as the first ever full-time schools worker in Leeds. This was just a month after I had got married to Clare and we moved into our new rented accommodation in Leeds.

Since then I have worked with Leeds Faith In Schools (continuing with HOG until 1996). Now I run www.2turntables.co.uk which is a network of DJs (some of them Christian) who train and pray with each other in the dance music scene. I do DJ workshops with young people and all the other things that schools workers do.

I am a keen basketball player, although not a very good one, being only 5′9″! I play with HASSRA, a local league team, and we also have the Youth for Christ FLY team basketball team in Leeds. This was a dream of mine (and Jon Burns) for years.

In 1995 I went to a conference called Remix in London which was for youth church people and people who were looking for a move of God among young people. It came off the back of a youth event in Leeds called Xpose, which hadn't worked very well, and I was looking for something else. I went to this conference and it completely changed my life, my walk with God and the way that I think about church and reaching out to young people. As Martin Smith says in one of his songs, 'I felt like the rug had been pulled from beneath my feet.'

The conference was amazing, it was just full of prophetic symbolism and it was a real release for me to have this mad time. From then I have never looked back and always seek to do things in a relevant but radical way if possible.

I am married to Clare and we have two daughters, Rhea and Lauren who were born in 1999. I go to Dayspring Church in Leeds.

Who Is Baz Gascoyne Anyway?

Baz is married to Linda and they will be celebrating their tenth wedding anniversary this December. They live and work in Sheffield.

Baz is originally from Darlington, County Durham, and moved south to Sheffield in 1986 to work for the YMCA as their Christian Outreach Worker. After nearly seven years, he moved on to work for a church as their evangelist.

Six years ago Linda and Baz planted a church in the community where they live. It began in their front room with a dozen people, but for the last four years has been meeting in the local community centre.

Baz's three main passions are first to communicate the gospel of Jesus in a relevant, humorous and non-religious way, whether it be at school assemblies, among students, churches, friends and neighbours or those who are 'Not Yet Christians'. Second, to give opportunities to people to have a go at things and discover their calling and gifting, and not wait until they are old! Third, to break the thinking of church people that until they become involved in full-time

Christian work they will always be second-class Christians. Baz says, 'We need people to be full-time Christians in the place where they live, study, work, play and drink, for this is full-time Christian work!'

Resources

A church that refuses to use contemporary culture to communicate the gospel will bring converts into a time warp. (Martin Robinson, *Idea* magazine Nov/Dec 2001)

The following we found helpful or thought provoking.

Books

20 Hot Potatoes Christians Are Afraid to Touch, Tony Campolo (Word)

50 Outlines for Men's Meetings, Dave Roberts and Howard Lewis (Kingsway)

An Enemy Called Average, John Mason (Honor Books)

Baton Change, Peter Lyne (Sovereign World)

Carpe Diem: Seize the Day, Tony Campolo (Word)

Church for the Unchurched, George Hunter (Abingdon Press)

Divine Appointments, Larry Tomczak (Destiny Image)

E.male Prayers for the Lads, Dave Gatward (Kevin Mayhew)

Feeding Your Forgotten Soul, Paul Borthwick (Zondervan)
Futurewise, Patrick Dixon (HarperCollins)
Hearing Men's Voices, Roy McCloughry (Hodder & Stoughton)
Hot Illustrations for Youth Talks, Wayne Rice (Youth Specialities)
How to Reach Secular People, George Hunter (Abingdon Press)
Man and Boy, Tony Parsons (HarperCollins)
Manhood, Steve Biddulph (Hawthorn Press)
Memory Makers, Doug Fields and Duffy Robbins (Zondervan)
Men and Masculinity, Roy McCloughry (Hodder & Stoughton)
Men Behaving Boldly, Paul Wallis (Triangle)
Men in Search of Their Soul, Roy McCloughry (Hodder & Stoughton)
Mind Games, Simon Hall (Scripture Union)
Operation World, Patrick Johnstone and Jason Mandryk (OM Publications)
Red Hot Ice Breakers, Michael Puffet and Sheldon W. Rottler (Monarch)
Revolutionary Christians Who Live the Gospel, Claire Richards (Kevin Mayhew)
Soul Survivor, Philip Yancey (Hodder & Stoughton)
Sowing, Reaping, Keeping, Lawrence Singlehurst (Crossway Books)
Sowing Seeds for Revival, Martin Scott (Sovereign World)
The Church Is Bigger Than You Think, Patrick Johnstone (Christian Focus)
The God Chasers, Tommy Tenney (Authentic Publishing)
The Man in the Mirror, Patrick M. Morley (Word)

The Message by Eugene Peterson (NavPress)
The McDonaldization of Church, John Drane (Longman & Todd)
The Sixty-Minute Father, Rob Parsons (Hodder & Stoughton)
The Snare, Lois Mowday (Navpress)
Was Jesus a Moderate?, Tony Campolo (Word)
We Must Stop Meeting Like This, Meic Pearse and Chris Matthews (Kingsway)
Whose Child Is This?, Bill Wilson (Charisma House)

Videos / Films / TV

All Quiet on the Western Front
Armageddon
As Good As It Gets
Billy Elliott
Braveheart
DC Talk Live in Concert
Erin Brockovich
Father of the Bride
Fight Club
Forrest Gump
Four Weddings and a Funeral
Freak Show
Gladiator
Good Morning Vietnam
Good Will Hunting
He Got Game
Hoop Dreams
Jerry McGuire
Leap of Faith

Liar Liar
Parenthood
Patch Adams
Philadelphia
Saving Private Ryan
Shadowlands
The Basketball Diaries
The Blues Brothers
The Fast Show Series 2 Part 2
The Fifth Element
The Fugitive
The Full Monty
The Godfather
The Green Mile
The Patriot
The Royle Family
The Simpsons – Heaven and Hell
The Truman Show
The Very Best of Father Ted
The Wedding Singer
The Wonder Years
Unforgiven
White Men Can't Jump

Websites

www.24-7prayer.com
www.2turntables.co.uk
www.damaris.org
www.LFIS.org
www.licc.org

50 Outlines for Men's Meetings

by Howard Lewis and Dave Roberts

The church has long understood the benefit of gathering men together in small groups. Jesus gathered his disciples in this way. John Wesley proved the value of allowing men to help and challenge one another. Today is no different.

The 50 outlines in this book will allow men to discover principles that will help shape their character in the following areas:

- their relationship with God
- home and family
- the workplace
- the wider community
- church

A focused approach to conversational learning will enable men to share stories of faith, reflect on Scripture, receive instruction and pray together.

How to be an Effective Father

by Ian Grant

Busy parents don't always have time or energy to be creative at home, but we all know that children need a good relationship with their dads.

Here, in one easy-to-read book, are user-friendly game plans that dads can put into practice with immediate results. These strategies are positive, practical and fun, based on years of experience in helping parents change the atmosphere in their homes.

Ian Grant demonstrates how men can become the consistent and loving fathers their children need. Written in short, easily-mastered sections, it includes practical advice for

- busy dads to connect with their children
- dads who don't live with their children
- having fun with your kids
- discipline that makes sense
- being a hero to your kids

Sons of the Father

by Gordon Dalbey

In recent times men have been told that they must

- relate to women in a healthier way
- take more initiative as fathers
- overcome their addictions and other destructive behaviours
- become men of strong family-based principles

The problem is, men learn these things from other men, namely from Dad. And dads are imperfect, or often absent. Some are even abusive.

Gordon Dalbey offers men a deeper understanding of the 'father wound', and clears a path for healing through a restored relationship with Father God.

"A great resource and discussion generator for our men's groups."

Steve Restrick
Founder/Senior Pastor, North Leeds Vineyard

"A truly amazing and life-changing book! The message of this book is needed more than ever in an increasingly fatherless world."

Brian Doerksen, Worship leader and songwriter